WRITERS' WORKSHOP SERIES

How to teach poetry writing at key stage 3

PIE CORBETT

David Fulton Publishers

London

David Fulton Publishers Ltd
The Chiswick Centre, 414 Chiswick High Road, London W4 5TF

www.fultonpublishers.co.uk

First published in Great Britain by David Fulton Publishers 2002

British Library Publication Data
A catalogue record for this book is available from the British Library

ISBN 1-85346-915-7

Also available in the **Writers' Workshop Series:**

How to teach poetry writing at key stage 2   ISBN 1-85346-804-5
How to teach fiction writing at key stage 2   ISBN 1-85346-833-9
How to teach writing across the curriculum at key stage 2   ISBN 1-85346-803-7

How to teach fiction writing at key stage 3   ISBN 1-85346-858-4
How to teach non-fiction writing at key stage 3   ISBN 1-85346-859-2

Cover photographs by John Redman
Typeset by FiSH Books, London

Contents

Acknowledgements

The publishers would like to thank the following copyright holders for permission to include their material:

James Berry, for an extract from 'Childhood Tracks' from *Playing a Dazzler*, published by Puffin, 1996. Reprinted by permission of Penguin Books Ltd.

Carcanet Press, for 'The Red Wheelbarrow' and 'This is Just to Say' by William Carlos Williams.

Pie Corbett, for 'Memory Senses' from *Writers' Source Book*, published by Heinemann, © Pie Corbett 2001 (under the pseudonym Peter Bicot); 'Message for the Mice that Live in the Roof' and 'Message for the Mosquito who Shares my Bedroom' from *The Hamster's Diary*, ed. Brian Moses, published by Oxford University Press, © Pie Corbett 1993; 'The Wolf's Wife Speaks' from *The Rhyme Riot*, published by Macmillan, © Pie Corbett 2002; 'One Line Riddles' and 'What Am I?' from *The Works 2*, published by Macmillan, © Pie Corbett 2002; 'An Odd Kettle of Fish' from *Rice, Pie and Moses* by John Rice, Pie Corbett and Brian Moses, published by Macmillan, © Pie Corbett 1995; 'Animal Riddle' from *Wacky Wild Animals*, ed. Brian Moses, published by Macmillan, © Pie Corbett 2000; 'Take Two' from *The Apple Raid*, published by Macmillan, © Pie Corbett 2001; 'Goodnight Stroud' from *Key Stage 3 Sentence Starters for Year 8*, published by Badger Publishing, © Pie Corbett 2001; 'Who's that on the Phone?' from *The Works 2*, published by Macmillan (also appeared in a Scholastic Magazine), © Pie Corbett 2000; 'City Jungle' from *Rice, Pie and Moses* by John Rice, Pie Corbett and Brian Moses, published by Macmillan Children's Books (also appeared in *GCSE, Key Stage 2 Welsh SATs* and National Literacy Strategy KS3 training materials), © Pie Corbett 1995. All other poems and fragments © Pie Corbett 2002. Children's poems previously appeared in school anthologies. Ideas on the Poetry Repertoire were first explored in an article for *The Times Educational Supplement*, © Pie Corbett 2001. Many thanks to the editors of the original publications where the above poems were first used.

Carol Ann Duffy, for 'Meeting Midnight' from *Meeting Midnight*, published by Faber and Faber, 1999; and an extract from 'The Oldest Girl in the World' from *The Oldest Girl in the World*, published by Faber and Faber, 2000.

Faber and Faber Ltd, for 'In a Station of the Metro' by Ezra Pound, from *Personae*, published in 1924, and for 'Thirteen Ways of Looking at a Blackbird' by Wallace Stevens, from *Collected Poems*.

Harcourt Inc., for 'Fog' by Carl Sandburg, from *Chicago Poems*, © 1914 by Holt, Rinehart and Winston, and renewed 1944 by Carl Sandburg.

David Kitchen, for 'A Fistful of Pacifists' from *Never Play Leapfrog with a Unicorn*, published by William Heinemann, 1995.

Adrian Mitchell, for an extract from 'Stufferation' from *Adrian Mitchell's Greatest Hits*, published by Bloodaxe Books, 1991. Reprinted by permission of PFD on behalf of Adrian Mitchell.

Brian Moses, for an extract from 'Jellyfish', from *Hippopotamus Dancing*, published by Cambridge University Press, © Brian Moses 1994.

Brian Patten, for 'Tiger Shadows' from *Juggling with Gerbils*, published by Puffin, 2000. Reprinted by permission of Rogers, Coleridge and White on behalf of Brian Patten.

Penguin Books Ltd, for an extract from 'Poems of Solitary Delights' by Tachibana Akemi, from *The Penguin Book of Japanese Verse*, translated by Geoffrey Bownas and Anthony Thwaite (Penguin Books 1964, revised edition 1998). Translation copyright © Geoffrey Bownas and Anthony Thwaite, 1964, 1998. Reprinted by permission of Penguin Books Ltd.

Kit Wright, for 'Magic Box' from *Cat Among Pigeons*, published by Viking Kestrel, 1987. Reprinted by permission of PFD on behalf of Kit Wright.

While the publishers have made every effort to contact copyright holders of previously published material in this volume, they would be grateful to hear from any they were unable to contact.

Introduction

Anyone setting out to write this sort of book will inevitably make a personal selection. There are so many possibilities when it comes to developing young writers and we all have our own favourite poetry workshops. I have selected a few old chestnuts that enthusiasts will be familiar with and included many others that have also worked well in many different classrooms. The more I listed ideas for workshops, the more I accumulated. Opportunities for writing ideas seemed endless. Sad then that so much which passes for English teaching is pedestrian and has little to do with engaging children as writers, creative beings with souls. Sad too for the teacher – for surely one of the most exciting aspects of teaching poetry writing is that it so directly involves our own creativity and imagination. I hope that this book contributes to making our classrooms dynamic places where communities of writers develop together.

I would place the teacher in that community. Successful teachers of English invariably write (and read) themselves. Whatever workshop you are running, having written your own poem will help you to check the pitfalls – after all, if you find it hard to do, so will your pupils. Your own poetry can be used as a model. It helps if you can share drafts, and talk through your own joys and struggles as a writer. One of the difficulties seems to be that some degrees in English are more about reading than writing, and teacher training courses pay insufficient attention to developing young teachers as writers. I am sure that your ability to read and write will deepen your own understanding of the process of creativity in the classroom.

Using the book

- I have provided a brief account of a 'writing repertoire' that might be developed across key stage 3, plus some general principles concerning running poetry workshops.
- There is a bank of poetry/language games. These are intended to act as creative ways to stimulate the imagination, to loosen up the necessary sense of playfulness that poetry requires, to encourage exploration and invention, and to introduce aspects of poetic language.

- The main body of the book is a series of poetry workshops, occasionally accompanied by a poem, or activity, that may be photocopied.
- There are some photocopiable sheets that may be used to provide advice to young writers.
- I have appended some suggested resources – if you read the few recommended books I believe you will be in a strong position to teach poetry effectively (see this book as part of that body of writing about poetry writing).

The poetic repertoire

Over time, young writers should be introduced to a range of possibilities – different techniques, strategies, forms, approaches and poetic possibilities. Across key stage 3 they may acquire an ever-broadening repertoire of writing techniques that they could use within their own poetry writing (and narrative). Most poetry teaching does not set out with the same intentions. It sets out to 'do a short unit on poetry' – read a bit and write a bit. I am more concerned with the gradual development of young writers, acquiring forms and techniques so that, ultimately, they can draw upon their poetic repertoire, making their decisions and choices for their own poems and stories.

Let us take a quick look at some aspects that might fall within this idea of an ever-increasing and sophisticated poetic repertoire. Here are some of the things that poems can do and that could become a part of their writing storehouse.

Comparison – similes/metaphors

Comparisons are sometimes the only way that experience can be communicated powerfully. They take a step further on from mere explanation. 'I dreamed about an amazing place' is no real substitute for reading 'Kubla Khan'. Comparisons bring experiences alive, making them memorable by dragging in other senses and ideas. At their best, comparisons should be fresh so that the reader looks anew at the experience. Only last week a seven-year-old boy came up with the image 'as thin as a bumble bee's wing', which contains a sense of frailty and beauty. Similes come in the form of 'like' or 'as' – both should be a regular part of the writer's repertoire.

Similes are obvious. But metaphors are sneaky and often more powerful. They transform the world, working on the reader in a less blatant way than similes. They are cunning beasts! 'The flimsy moon has lost her wits' (Ted Hughes).

Personification and apostrophe

Bringing the world alive by using personification is a powerful poetic device. It helps the writer get closer to the subject and is especially useful for creating atmosphere (the wind moaned) and surprise (the kettle whispered).

So too does apostrophe – a way of addressing the world. Blake used this to talk to tigers. It helps to draw in all sorts of close possibilities and connections so that anything can be addressed – the moon, death, God... 'Batter my heart, three-personned God' (John Donne).

Juxtaposition

Juxtaposition is one of the most powerful writing tools available to a poet. Avoiding the weary combination or the tired cliché can help to bring a spark of truth to a situation that makes the reader sit up and pay attention. For instance, it may be easy enough to write 'the old lady hobbled', but it is more powerful to pause, think and then produce a more unusual combination, 'the old lady break-danced'.

Lying

Poets do this all the time, from pretending that their love is like a rose through to fabricating whole tales. The best form of lying strikes at a truth: 'She walks in beauty, like the night...'(Lord Byron). Of course, this is a special form of lie. Lying not to deceive but to illuminate: 'A mouthful of silence' (David Kitchen).

Pretending

Poets constantly pretend – to know, to understand, to conceal, to reveal, to invent. 'White bird featherless, flew from paradise' (anon.). No it didn't – it snowed! 'The wolf inside my pocket is hungry' (Helen Dunmore).

Questions and exclamations

Questions are useful to help you address the world, to ask the obvious or the unlikely. 'What immortal hand or eye,/could frame thy fearful symmetry?' (William Blake). They can help to open up a subject. 'Mummy, is his tummy black?' (James Berry).

Exclamations are good for sounding off. 'Poor beastie, thou maun live!' (Robbie Burns).

Synesthesia

This a useful technique and involves talking about one sense in relation to another, for example, 'I want to paint the scent of the sun's first ray'.

Boasting and exaggeration

This is lovely device. To be able to really show off, to cut a swagger with words, to become more than we are. 'I am a green bear...I do not roar and snarl like other bears/I sing' (Richard Edwards). 'I am writing these lines/from inside a lion' (Shel Silverstein).

Advising and commenting

In the realm of poetry advice can be dished out to all sorts – people, animals, objects, fantasy, feelings, eternity. 'Tap me with your finger/rub me with your sleeve' (Edwin Morgan). The writer can feel free to comment on, or speak for, the world. 'Such a peculiar lot/we are; we people/without money' (James Berry).

Telling secrets

In a sense poetry is all about revealing secrets. Of course we can be inventive and reveal secrets that have never been told before. 'Stones dream of having warm hearts/too long they have been cold' (Pie Corbett). 'Pomegranites do not feel pain' (Helen Dunmore).

Making poetic the ordinary

This is a matter of taking the everyday and casting it anew. 'The window's eyes are glazed with constant staring' (George Szirtes).

Making it musical

The rhythm, rhymes and sound effects may conspire to make a poem memorable and beautiful beyond all reason. 'Inky pinky ponky/Daddy had a donkey./The donkey died/Daddy cried./Inky pinky ponky' (anon.). ''Twas brillig and the slithy toves/did gyre and gimble in the wabe' (Lewis Carroll).

Finally, there are a lot more points that we could add to this repertoire – but this seems like a good list of possibilities for key stage 3.

Many of these workshops are rather like poetry-grammar exercises. They introduce young writers to a range of possibilities and techniques. Those of us who have worked intensively with young writers can testify to the way in which this repertoire may be built up through such workshops. I noticed quickly in my teaching that if I introduced similes early on in the year then in other sessions, where the focus was elsewhere, similes would creep in. I realised that some children were gathering a range of techniques and approaches that they could draw upon in their own writing. I began to isolate an ongoing 'poetic checklist' of techniques. They are as follows.

How to make pictures in the reader's mind

- Choosing the right word – to illuminate;
- Similes – to build pictures;
- Metaphors – to transform;
- Personification – to bring scenes alive and create atmosphere;
- Varying word order – to surprise the reader.

How to make sound effects

- Alliteration – making phrases memorable;
- Onomatopoeia – reflecting and adding to meaning;
- Rhymes – making memorable echoes.

How to make the poem visually effective

- Shape – reflects or adds to the meaning of the poem;
- Pattern – helps the reader and gives emphasis to words/meaning.

It seems to me that as a writer I am still building up this repertoire. Sometimes I take a leap forward on my own through constant investigation and experimentation; at other times I add to my own repertoire through reading other writers, and their poems strengthen or introduce me to new ideas. The process is never ending.

Reading as a writer

It would take many years to pick up all of this by haphazard reading. However, a well-constructed programme of reading can help to speed up the process. Young writers can be introduced to these ideas if the teacher is consciously aware of the need to build up the range of writing possibilities. In this book I have leaned towards discussing the teaching of writing. However, this is inextricably linked to reading.

A complete programme needs to link the reading, performing, listening and writing of poetry in a cycle. We need to touch on one important idea here. You can speed up the development of young writers by helping them to 'read as writers', as artists. This means learning how to look at poems as artefacts – to respond as a reader, losing oneself in the text, and then to step back and gaze at the poem, wondering: how was that effect created? I think all writers do this – probably anyone serious about their art has a fascination in what others do and how they did it. Thus a powerful strategy for broadening the writing repertoire is built around looking at quality examples of poetry and teasing out how the writer has gained effects, what techniques or forms are being used and so on.

A strong element of this comes through exposure to writers. Schools where writing matters have found ways to work with writers both in school and often on residential trips. I have included a few brief thoughts about this in the Appendix, but I mention it here because not everything can be picked up from looking at a poem. We can see the form, the techniques – but we cannot find out much about 'how' the writer set about it. In the course of this book I have included many pointers about writing that I have picked up from other poets/authors. While there are differences in approach there are also certain commonalities that we can draw upon.

The writing journal

One key aspect that is common to every poet whom I have met is that they keep some form of writing journal. Some recent work that I have carried out in year 6 classes has demonstrated that even quite young writers can use journals to aid their writing.

My own writing journals (and I have about 30) act for me in a number of ways.

- I jot down ideas – it is easy to forget ideas (how many times has a pupil had an idea, put up their hand and then in the next second forgotten it?). Ideas are slippery customers and need to be well netted or they may get lost. So, if I get an idea I jot it down on the back of my hand, on a scrap of paper, on my cheque book – anywhere. Then in the evening I note it in my journal. In this way the journal becomes a storehouse of writing ideas.
- I test run poems/prose, using the journal as a

place for initial drafts. It is worth noting that quite a lot of these are doodles and come to nothing.

- It is where I 'practise'. If you want to become good at anything, practise is essential. Marathon runners work out in the gym, run short bursts, go swimming and so on. You cannot just get up one day and go out and run a Marathon. Well, writers are the same – you get better by practising (and being taught also helps).
- In the journal I plan, plot, brainstorm, list.
- I note down:
  - words which spring to mind that might be part of a poem/story;
  - things I see and are unusual or striking;
  - things I overhear;
  - fragments of dreams;
  - ideas for stories/poems;
  - quotes from other writers.

In school young writers may get used to gathering ideas, testing them out and so forth in a journal. It may be handy to use the journal in two other ways. First, I have noticed that in some writing sessions pupils like to take notes – jotting down words and ideas during the pre-writing discussion. This can mean that by the time they come to write they have already gathered some embryonic thinking for their writing. Second, the back of the journal may be used to list – as a reminder – aspects of poetic technique and the repertoire as they are introduced. This part of the journal may then be referred to by pupils when writing – a reminder of the possibilities that might be drawn upon. This could also contain snippets of advice about writing, gleaned from meeting different writers.

The journal opens up the possibility of pupils beginning to become writers as a matter of course. One of the biggest weapons we have as teachers is to show interest in what our pupils are up to. I like to share my own journals, show drafts of poems, write alongside pupils – to try to establish a writerly atmosphere. Let us take this writing business seriously – after all, one of our main roles as English teachers is to develop young writers.

Inspiration

Before we move on to discuss a few principles about running writing workshops I want to say something about that most awkward customer – inspiration. I do think that this is a tough nut to

crack, especially in school. Writers find their own ways to get into a 'writing mood' – we can easily create a writing atmosphere and get to know the things that trigger us. George MacBeth wrote at night with his feet up – he claimed the blood rushing to his head helped him write. Michael Morpurgo likes to lie on his bed and often tells his stories aloud into a recorder. I have certain pieces of music that help me to slip into writing mood. Many writers like to walk if they get stuck, and in some way this helps to unblock and release a new flow.

We have all tried in school to teach writing, battling against a din from the class next door. We can help to set the mood – music helps, as establishing a quiet, receptive, trusting atmosphere is necessary. But for me the key has to be feelings. We write best about what we know (our experience) and what matters to us. This means that the starting points for writing have to connect in both ways.

- What we know – this implies that the subjects need to either fall within our common experience (writing about thunder storms, for instance) or the teacher has to provide the experience (e.g. bringing in a ship in a bottle).
- What matters – this implies that the subjects for writing need to touch a nerve. They may be playful, and the interest comes through the invitation to play with language and create inventive ideas. They may be subjects close to experiences that are connected with emotion, such as moving house or school. They may be related to pupils' own interests and passions. They may be related to stimulating curiosity through using firsthand experience – bringing into the classroom objects, works of art and so on.

My experience is that if you find starting points that fire the class up, then, with the wind in the right direction, many pupils will feel that touch of inspiration. But the ideas have to fall within their experience, and to interest, excite, intrigue and touch their feelings.

Running a workshop

Secondary schools are not always designed to allow sufficient time and space for creativity. What on earth can be done with three 'lessons' a week, lasting 35 minutes each plus a separate lesson called 'literacy' (which turns out to be grammar divorced from the act of reading and writing and therefore another pointless waste of time)? So, I understand the constraints and frustrations, and all I can do is summarise a few pointers and leave you to lobby, push, plead, persuade, cajole (appeal to the heart and mind) as far as you can to provide sufficient time and a positive environment for creativity to have a chance to flourish.

A few underlying principles:

- Create a supportive atmosphere – try to establish a sense of mutual respect. Some days great poems just seem to arrive – on others it becomes a formulaic exercise.
- Poems can be taken away and worked on.
- Specific sessions are needed to teach 'polishing' the poem (revising).
- Sometimes you find an idea begins to grow – follow it. You do not always have to follow the direction that has been set up. Get used to noticing when a different avenue is fruitful.
- Poetry is a serious game – it needs a disciplined focus when writing, but it also needs a playfulness.
- As I have already stated, I believe the teacher needs to be a reader/writer of poetry themselves.

Poetry games

Many workshops benefit from starting with a quick game. I have listed a number of games I have collected over the years (and I am grateful to various teachers, poets, workshop leaders who have unwittingly contributed to the list). I see the games as a way of grabbing the class by the scruff of the neck and engaging their creativity immediately. The games tend to be playful, breaking down conventions and clichés. Often they introduce an aspect of poetic writing that may be used in the main body of the session – or just revisit a technique. I see the games as linguistic 'warm-ups', syntactical gymnastics, creative fine-tuning. I think too that they help to strengthen the imagination. It just is not good enough to suggest that a pupil – or class – is unimaginative. One of our roles as teachers of English is to strengthen the ability to imagine, and these games help.

Starting point

We have already noted how important it is to find a focus for writing that will fall within the pupils'

experience and also fire them up. This may mean using a clutch of poems, a model poem, developing a game further, using objects, music, art work, a visit, recalling an experience and so forth. This book provides workshop ideas – and books in the Recommended Resources section contain many hundreds of other ideas. Writing ideas should be:

1 within their experience;
2 it must 'matter' – excite, intrigue, amuse, move;
3 you need a clear focus.

Discussion

This may involve using questions to trigger thinking/wondering, drawing attention to an experience, encouraging pupils to pinpoint details. It helps if the class becomes used to making notes during this time. Words and ideas may well flicker into mind and will be lost if not noted down.

Brainstorm/listing

These are the main techniques that need teaching. Whole-class brainstorms, word webs or lists are a useful demonstration of how to dredge up words and ideas. This needs to be rapid – say 10 minutes – and a time for looking/thinking carefully about the subject and digging deep for appropriate words to illuminate the experience. Push the class to become swift 'wordsearchers'.

I sometimes see this activity rather like hopping across stepping-stones over a stream. One word is contributed. Then push the class to take it a step further. For instance, if the word 'red' comes up this could lead quickly on – red – scarlet – crimson. If you do not push, the brain does not develop this ability to swiftly generate choices, to sift and filter a team of words. Regular brainstorming trains this ability.

If I could count the number of times I have been told that 'the children do not have a good vocabulary', I would be a rich man. In the main, this is a nonsense and has to be resisted. Whatever next – children who are unimaginative, not creative? The problem is not so much lack of vocabulary; it is a matter of gaining access to the vocabulary they know, understand but do not often use in everyday speech. Good writing does not need 'big' words – it needs well-chosen words. It needs words that bring experiences alive, words that work – grip, grab, grasp, cling, stab, scrape, scratch and so on. These are not words that are out of the ken of most pupils. It is just a matter of gaining access to the words – that is why constant brainstorming is important. For those who struggle, the act of constantly collecting vocabulary and ideas helps pupils to draw upon the breadth of their full vocabulary. (Intriguingly, I have yet to meet a special needs department that spent much time on any of this sort of work – they labour on trying to develop children's writing through regular doses of spelling and grammar.)

Ultimately, perhaps quite rapidly, you can move to a position where pupils make their own brainstorms on some occasions. But do not drop the whole-class approach. Creative avenues often trigger off other people's ideas.

Shared writing

I still believe that the central aspect of teaching writing is shared writing. If you do not do shared writing in some form then you are not teaching writing. You may be getting them to write – but there is a difference between teaching writing and setting up situations in which writing occurs.

I use two different tactics (or a combination of both):

1 *Demonstration* – I write the poem (or part of it) myself, giving a running commentary on what is happening – describing what I am thinking as I am composing.
2 *Shared composition* – we draft the poem together, sifting ideas and words with pupils making suggestions. I try to challenge them to strengthen ideas if they are weak and talk through why one way seems to be more effective than another.

One further dimension worth trying is to rapidly produce a rough draft of a poem and then invite the class to develop and polish it on their own. This can produce interesting variations and provides good practice in honing a poem.

Independent writing

The shift into writing needs to be swift. At this point the class needs to be ready to write – bubbling with ideas, clear about what needs to be done. The last thing you want at this point is a knock at the door and for somebody selling poppies to appear. I like the class to write in total silence and rapidly. The aim is for the writer to

become absorbed in the writing – so absorbed that everything else is blocked out and the full beam of the creative intelligence is focused upon the creation of the poem. This means writing rapidly with fierce concentration.

I usually provide a time limit of about 10 minutes. I may let this run on if the class is engrossed. But, generally, I do not give long periods of time. Ted Hughes writes about this sort of meditative concentration in *Poetry in the Making*. His basic premise is that if you tap into your inner intelligence, the writing will flow – and often a whole poem appears. This is quite true – I have seen it happen many times. He goes on to make the point that if you lose concentration, wander about and start to worry about the words, the worry sets in and will kill the spirit of the poem. It is an interesting combination – we ask for a disciplined, concentrated focus during writing that is balanced by the invitation to play, experiment, invent, be a little crazy with language and not to worry.

Worry is the enemy of creativity. Again, I have seen it a thousand times. A few words are written, the writer pauses, the pen leaves the page and hovers – and nothing happens. The writer rereads, mistrust sets in – it does not sound any good, I cannot do this, what should I put next . . . and the poem dies.

Drafting

This may occur during a session, at home or in the next session. Pupils work in pairs or individually, polishing their writing. The exhortation to 'add more' usually leads to spoiling the writing by embellishing too much.

I think that demonstrating how to polish a poem is vital. This may be your own, a class version or indeed have reference to poems, or parts of poems, written by some of the class (if some children draft straight on to an OHT this can provide a simple focus for whole-class teaching of revision). You are looking for what sounds clumsy or ugly, repetition that has no effect, clichés, verbs that might be made more powerful, adjectives that add little, clumsy phrasing and so forth.

I like to leave the final decisions to the writer – though as a class we might make suggestions about strengths and areas to work upon.

Reading/publishing

There is much to be said for pupils getting used to reading their poetry aloud – to a partner, a small group or the class. Again, every poet whom I know reads their work aloud. It is the testing ground, for it enables the writer to listen as a reader to what has been written. Often it is through reading aloud that pupils can see and hear silly errors as well as parts that are clumsy or do not flow. Pupils know the truth of this – they have all had the experience of being asked to come to the front of class and read their work out loud. Half-way through, the eye spots a missing word or some other such glitch – so what do they do? Change it of course, because we all know that writing should make sense – and good sense, if possible.

Years ago I remember producing class anthologies on the school Banda. While some colleagues loved the sniff of alcohol, it had to be faced – the end results were not very impressive. With the advent of photocopying it should have become increasingly simple to publish poems regularly. Class and school anthologies should be a regular part of the work of the English department. And never underestimate such simple ideas as printing A3 posters of poems to pin up in different places around the school. (I will never forget finding a copy of 'Kubla Khan' in the staff toilets in one secondary school!)

Poetry Games – Syntactic Gymnastics

Poetry games are a good way to warm up the word, to exercise and strengthen the imagination. In no particular order, here are various games that I have gathered over the years (I am grateful to all those teachers, poets and writers who introduced me to different ideas).

Whiteboard games

Use mini-whiteboards. Build on the following ideas:

- Give the class one to four words to make up a sentence, e.g. *jelly, shark, whispered.*
- Provide a word, e.g. *cat* and the class have to write a sentence using alliteration – or a simile using like or as, or a metaphor or personification.
- Write down a dull sentence and ask the class to make it live, e.g. *The cat went along the thingy = The snooty Siamese break-danced on the bannisters.*
- Ask the class to write a sentence, e.g. *The horse ran down the bank.*
- Now to take out the verb – how does it sound?
- Now add back in the verb and some adjectives or an adverb, e.g. *The red horse ran rapidly down the steep bank.*
- Now take out the nouns, e.g. *The red ran rapidly down the steep.*
- Now extend it using 'because', e.g. *The red ran rapidly down the steep because it was thirsty.*
- Shift the end to the beginning, e.g. *Because it was thirsty, the red ran rapidly down the steep.*
- Shift the adverb, e.g. *Rapidly, because it was thirsty, the red ran down the steep.*
- Keep on playing in this manner, making up sentences, listening to the impact. Add in techniques such as alliteration, similes, personification.
- Provide two or three short sentences. Link them together, e.g. *The dog barked. The burglar ran. The lorry stopped. = As soon as the lorry stopped, the dog barked because the burglar ran.*
- Provide a short sentence and ask the class to make it longer (or vice versa).

- Provide sentence fragments that have to be completed, e.g. *rushed crazily = The diamonds rushed crazily through my hair.*
- Keep it swift, lively and creative. Challenge language and listen to its effects.

Word swap

Select a sentence from any book. Swap words over to create new and surreal effects, e.g. *I brushed into the bathroom and stroked my teeth.*

Metaphor game

Choose an animal and compare it to a person, a place, an object, a mood, a colour, e.g. *It is an oak table late at night.*

Ink waster

In one minute list as many words as you can think of to do with a particular subject or write as much as you can about that subject.

Strange word combinations

Take a word and list as many adjectives and verbs that might go with it. Go for the most unlikely combination, e.g. *cruel ink, silent ink, sad ink.*

Nonsense words

Invent nonsense words. Swap with a friend. Create nonsense sentences using the words you have been given, e.g. *The brumly tubhip was dinating by the condly pirostin.*

Rhythm games

Clap, echo sounds and words, repeat sounds rhythmically.

Pass the poem

Take a poem with a repeating pattern and pass it around the room, adding ideas, e.g. *'At the end of the rainbow I saw…'.*

Free association

Provide a word, e.g. *snow, flame, sea.* The class has one minute to list as many words as possible –

almost without thinking. The secret is to not worry and let the words flow.

In the street I saw...

Pass around the class – orally – adding a new idea each time, to build a picture of a scene, e.g. *In the street I saw a bicycle, a post box, an old man falling over, a crashed car.*

Pie Corbett is...

Write a rapid list, boasting and inventing, e.g.

*Pie Corbett is
a ghost waiting on the second floor of a burnt out
   cinema,
a butcher slicing meat,
a shabby excuse,
a Mercedes at top speed,
a greedy hustler,
an undiscovered planet.*

Inventing family names

For example, *the Quentin-Sowerbutts, the Hogsworths, the Littlemarches, the Snuggs.*

Car or place names

Collect names of cars or places and invent rhymes, e.g.

*I got bored
In a Ford.*

Surreal games

At the recent surrealist exhibition in Tate Modern I picked up a number of surrealist games that would be of possible use in the classroom.

Automatic writing

Start writing and continue without thinking, writing as fast as you can. If you stop, start again immediately by using the last letter of the last word that you wrote as the first letter of the next word. Then continue. This could be timed for, say, two minutes.

The exquisite corpse (Consequences)

Pass around a piece of paper on which in turn you write a determiner, an adjective, a noun, a verb, an adverb, a preposition, an adjective, a noun. The game acquired its name from the first sentence obtained using this method (*The exquisite corpse shall drink the new wine*).

Question and answer

This is played in a similar way to Consequences, by writing and folding over a piece of paper to hide what has been written. The first player writes a question on a piece of paper and folds it over. The partner provides an answer. Obviously these will not match, but may provide some interesting chimes.

Conditionals

The same sort of idea as above, except that the first player writes a hypothetical sentence beginning with 'if' or 'when'. This is hidden and the partner writes a sentence in the conditional or future tense, e.g.

*If there were no swans
The snow would cover the porch.*

*If leopards lost their spots
The match would have to be postponed.*

Syllogisms

Similar to Conditionals but groups of three are needed. The first player writes down a proposition beginning with the word 'all'. The second player writes down a further proposition using the word 'there'. The third player writes a conclusion using the word 'therefore'. Each sentence is hidden by folding the paper, e.g.

*All clouds are damp.
There are no orchids on the moon.
Therefore the car will not start.*

Opposites

The first player writes down a statement. The second player looks at this statement and writes down the opposite, and then folds the first line to hide it. The third player then writes the opposite to the second line, then hides it and so on, e.g.

*The shiny moon rides in the dark night sky.
The dull sun sinks on the bright day's earth.
The gleaming pea swims below the shadowy
   night's air.*

Cut-ups

This can become quite creative if you provide some interesting material. I like to provide the following:

- A recipe card from Waitrose/Tesco, etc.
- A page from a holiday brochure.
- A page from a newspaper.

The game is quite simple. Cut up sentences and parts of sentences, clauses, phrases and words. Reassemble so that sentences syntactically make sense even if semantically they are sheer lunacy, e.g. *Take two slices of ham, nine tons of liquid oxygen and relax by the pool.*

Collages

A group of images that pile up to create a whole entity. Brian Moses and I used the expression in *Catapults and Kingfishers* (Oxford University Press) as a way of describing list poems: 'each line starts with the same phrases and all the writer has to do is to tack on a new idea each time', e.g.

The Room

I stood in a room full of computers
And caught a virus.

I stood in a room full of clocks
And my hands twitched.

I stood in a room full of hearts
And tapped out a steady beat.

I stood in a room full of mobile phones
& hd a txt msg.

Calligrams

Mini surprises – the word is written in such a way that it echoes or adds to the meaning of the word, e.g.

Alphabet games

There is a long tradition of alphabet books and counting rhymes. Both can be hijacked for writing. Alphabets are useful for exploring alliteration. Here are a number of quickfire ideas:

Alphabet events

Decide on a place and take your alphabet there. What does each letter do?

At the airport:

A ate a sandwich,
B bought a magazine,
C caught a plane.

Alphabet of ingredients

Make a simple list – for a holiday, a party, a school trip, e.g. *In a giant's kitchen I found*:

An antelope's tail, a baboon's banana. . . .

Alphabet of disasters

A was an avalanche crushing lives,
B was a bomb ticking away,
C was a crash.

Alphabet of people

Each letter links a name and an event.

Amy ate an ant!
Boris buried a bat!
Clare carved a canary!

Alphabet of places

Use an atlas to come up with what might happen in different places.

Spent a while
In Argyll.

Was quite cute
In Bute.

Won some cash
In Cat's Ash.

Felt free
In Dundee.

New definitions

Select one word for each letter of the alphabet and provide a poetic definition, e.g.

Answer – whatever is forever lingering alone on the tip of my tongue.
Ballet – the flutter of a whale's song.
Custom – the white bandage that stems the flow of freedom.

Animal numbers

What do the animals do?

One ant ambulates.
Two cats creep.
Three dogs dither.
Four eagles elongate.

St Ives counting rhyme

This idea is based upon the old rhyme, 'As I was going to St Ives I met a man with seven wives'.

While I was going to St Ives
I met a man with seven wives.

Each wife had six calves.
None of them did things by halves.

Each wife had five leaves.
Most of their goods, stolen by thieves.

Each wife had four knives.
Very handy for saving lives.

Each wife had three doves.
And fourteen pairs of scarlet gloves.

Each wife had crossed two roads.
Five were kind, but two had toads.

That is all I know of the one mystery man
Whom I passed, near St Ives, in his travelling van.

Pick and mix game

This game sometimes produces remarkable combinations – shafts of insight that might never have occurred. I provide a list of words in a bag, written on cards, perhaps set out like a bingo sheet, or on a web (a shape you cut out and fold into a box) – in some format that might intrigue. The game is simple enough.

- Select a given number of words (let us say five).
- Write a haiku (or some other form).
- Each word has to be used – though verbs may be adapted, nouns pluralised, etc.
- Further instructions might include other directions – you have to use the word 'like', you must alliterate, use personification, etc.

I usually start this session by demonstrating the idea myself. For instance from the words suggested below, I have selected the following five: moon print silk red kindle.

The moon prints a hoof.
Red poppies are black silk.
Flames kindle the hearth.

Some suggested words to use (or choose your own)

Moon print silk red kindle glass sharp sun mirror edge perfect shape cut night scarlet beak window door peak glare sullen jagged donkey clip raid grasp apple guide knife attic teeth green mild wind dig rain shot bees lock finger tip cheek dusk bloom perch glue blind eyes fidget yawn restless taxis shuffle bruise knuckle punch melt spin fire roar holler slip smooth egg blue.

Another version

In another version of this game I start with an empty box. This has to be filled with words, images, ideas. A starting point is needed; any clear image will do, preferably something tangible that can be seen – a key, a tower, a river, the night sky, a face, a bicycle, a fire, a candle, an explosion, etc. Photos, posters, slides, video clips are all helpful.

The box has to be filled with images. Ask the class what the subject is 'like' – What does it reminds them of? What does it look like? Accept everything, even the more bizarre, and fill the box. The ideas can then be strung together to form a sort of riddle based on a cairn of similes.

Alternatively, select one simile that seems to have the most potential. Turn this into a metaphor and extend the idea. For instance, one class I worked with suggested that stars looked like ants. We listed ideas about ants and then created the following.

Stars are ants
That scuttle across the dark
Face
Of the night
Tunnelling deep,
Creating mounds,
Touching gently with feelers
To guide the way.
Carrying a hundred times their weight,
Always busy.
Dashing along long lines
A calligraphy that cannot be read.

Manifold Manor

Philip Gross considered himself a poet for adults until Moira Andrews invited him into her primary school in Bristol. A month later he had written the whole book. It seems worth mentioning because it was one of the most remarkable poetry books published for young writers in the twentieth century. (Big claim: OK – you wait and see.) The writing is beautifully crafted and the poems offer mystery, suspense, invention, play, emotion, depth all wrapped up in a serious game.

The reader is invited to enter Manifold Manor. The poems visit different parts of the manor and we meet different characters. At the back of the book Philip invites the reader. *'If you want to make further discoveries, all you have to do is to write them for yourself. Several of the poems here are games that can be played again and again and come out different each time.'* My three favourite games are:

1 *The Twenty-Sixers.* This is an alphabet poem that begins:

> *An Angel Arguing with an Ancient Ape...*
> *A Bishop Breaking Bread with a Baboon.*

2 *Jack's Nature Study.* This is a riddle that begins:

> *Each of us a day –*
>> *long wink*
>> *back at the sun.*

3 *The Doors.* A series of poems about doors of different colours. These poems echo Miroslav Holub's poem 'The Door' which is another invitation to pass through a door and see what is on the other side.

The whole book calls for a visit to a local castle, old house, deserted place, museum, fire station, old cinema, whatever. Take notes. Jot down details. Dream up characters, dramatic events, whatever the place speaks. Use some of the games to create sequences of poems linked around a place. **Manifold Manor** is published by Faber.

1 Getting started

- Keep a poetry writing journal, notebook or diary. Jot down ideas for poems, things you notice, details, words, similes, things people say, observations, anything that occurs. Get into the habit of scribbling down ideas.

- Use music to get into a writing mood. Find a favourite place to write.

- Listen to your feelings, thoughts and dreams. Jot down thoughts as you daydream them. Keep a journal of your night-time dreams.

- Write inside or outside. Use your senses to listen, touch, smell, taste, look and wonder.

- Write about the following:
  - Pictures, photos, posters, postcards, old letters, diary extracts, film, sculptures, videos
  - Intriguing objects, collections, places, creatures, people, moments and events
  - Secrets, wishes, lies, hatreds, hopes, jealousies and dreams
  - Pretend to talk with and to people, places, objects, creatures ('Tyger, Tyger burning bright'), both real and imaginary
  - Write about your obsessions – what you feel passionately about, dream about, hate
  - Begin with what you know. Write about what is true, and what is not true but might be, as well as things which could never be true
  - Be outrageous – boast, exaggerate, plead, wonder, imagine, joke
  - Use memories of special moments – get used to noting your memories down, even if they are fleeting moments (if you remember something then it must be important – even a fragment can be significant).

- Write in different voices – as yourself or something else.

- Have a clear focus for writing. Do not be vague.

2 Before writing

● Look carefully at your subject. Stare at it, study the detail, seek out its truth. Visually and mentally make notes of the details.

● Become a 'wordsearcher' – before writing get used to brainstorming, listing, jotting ideas and words, whispering ideas in your mind. Create maps on the page with webs of words. Play with the words. (They never bite.)

3 Writing your poem

- Settle in a comfortable place to write with a favourite paper, pen, pencil.
- Remember that it does not always come out right at first – just start writing.
- The first draft may look messy as you try out words and ideas.
- Poems can be built up, adding a brick at a time, piling up images and ideas.
- Poems can be like jigsaws – you can move fragments around to find the best fit.
- Concentrate on choosing words with care – always test out alternatives to find the best combination.
- Write on every other line to give yourself space to add new ideas and make changes. Use a large piece of paper so that you have space.
- Use your writing journal, plus a thesaurus (a rhyming dictionary can be handy too).
- When you write, do not get distracted – concentrate hard or it will go wrong.
- Sift words and select the best from your mind. The first choice is not always the best choice – keep leaping from word to word.
- Look at the subject – try to hold it in your mind.
- Write quickly so that the poem flows – you can edit it later.
- Work from the brainstorm, selecting and discarding.
- Go for quality, not quantity.
- Avoid overwriting – especially using too many adjectives or adverbs. Try to find your voice – your way of doing things.
- Keep rereading as you write – mutter different possibilities to yourself and listen to it, think about it, and watch the poem's shape as it grows.
- Do not be afraid to take risks, try unusual ideas and words; do not always take the first word that occurs to you; pause and try out alternatives – poetry is about inventing.
- Play with the line breaks to make your writing look like a poem.
- Take a new line at a natural pause and to give emphasis.
- Create strong pictures by using similes, metaphors and personification.
- Create memorable sounds by using repetition for effect, alliteration, onomatopoeia, rhythm and rhyme.
- Create powerful poems by choosing precise nouns (*Rottweiler* not *dog*), necessary adjectives (*rusty* not *red* letterbox) powerful verbs (*mutter* not *talk*) and words that do not obviously go together so that you surprise the reader (not '*the old lady hobbled down the road*' but try '*the old lady jogged*').

4 After writing

- Read your poem aloud and listen to how it sounds – even if you are on your own. Often you will immediately notice places where it might be improved.

- Read your poem to a partner, poetry circle or the whole class – listen to their response and then take the time to work on it.

- Be a good response partner – read through, or listen to the writer read their poem. Always tell the writer what you liked first. Discuss any concerns the writer may have. Make a few positive suggestions.

- Poetry is about celebration and enjoyment – a serious game. Here are some ways to spread your poems around:

  - Perform to the class, other classes, the school

  - make a poetry programme or video

  - email or fax poems to other schools or put poems on the school website

  - publish in class anthologies, scrapbooks, homemade books, on poetry display boards

  - hold a poetry party performance, or make picturebook poems for a younger class

  - illustrate and create poetry posters

  - hold a poem swap

  - send poems to magazines (e.g. *Young Writer*), newspapers, literary websites, radio and TV.

The Poet's Repertoire

- Over time you will learn various different forms that you can select for different occasions (e.g. raps for entertaining, haiku for memorable moments, free verse for serious poems and capturing experiences).

- Being true to the experience that you are writing about is more important than trying to squeeze words into a form.

- To write in any form you need to spend time reading good poems written in that form.

- Read like a writer – notice how poets achieve different effects.

- Borrow simple repeating patterns from poets and invent your own (e.g. Kit Wright's 'The Magic Box').

- Invent your own forms and structures.

- Be careful with rhyme. Rhyme is handy for funny poetry and is easy enough when you have a strong pattern (e.g. Michael Rosen's 'Down Behind a Dustbin…'). But forcing a rhyme can lead to dishonest writing. Go for the right word rather than a forced rhyme.

- Keep the writing concrete and detailed.

- Use your own poetic voice. Try to use natural language and invent memorable speech – listen for this in everyday speech.

- Avoid old poetic language; use musical language.

Ways of Looking

Observation – firsthand experience

Learning to observe carefully, to watch the truth of experience, lies at the heart of many poets' writing. Ted Hughes believed that it was possible to capture the spirit of a poem by focusing our whole attention, absorbing ourselves meditatively in the subject, watching every detail so that the writer can capture and re-create an intimate image of the subject. His advice to young writers focuses upon this need to look carefully, to seek out the illuminating detail:

> imagine what you are writing about. See it and live it. Do not think it up laboriously, as if you were working out mental arithmetic. Just look at it, touch it, smell it, listen to it, turn yourself into it. When you do this, the words look after themselves, like magic.... You keep your eyes, your ears, your nose, your taste, your touch, your whole being on the thing you are turning into words. The minute you flinch, and take your mind off this thing, and begin to look at the words and worry about them...then your worry goes into them and they set about killing each other.
>
> (from *Poetry in the Making*, Ted Hughes, Faber 1967)

Hughes' advice to young writers is simple enough and could be summarised as:

- Use your senses to respond to your subject.
- Zoom in closely on the subject like a telephoto lens.
- Write quickly.
- Do not worry too much about the words as you write – try to write in a quick, concentrated flow.

In the same way Gerard Manley Hopkins' notebooks show how he used to become absorbed in an experience. He would filter through his mind a stream of words and images to attempt to re-create the experience. For him, it was a limbering-up exercise, an attempt to recapture the true essence of the experience, an intimate image. Here he is looking at raindrops:

> Drops of rain hanging on rails etc. seen with only the lower rim lighted like nails (of fingers). Screws of brooks and twines. Soft chalky look with more shadowy middles of the globes of cloud on a night with a moon faint or concealed. Mealy clouds with a not brilliant moon. Blunt buds of the ash. Pencil buds of the beech. Lobes of the trees. Cups of the eyes. Gathering back lightly hinged eyeballs. Bows of the eyelids. Pencil of eyelashes. Juices of the eyeball. Eyelids like leaves, petals, caps, tufted hats, handkerchiefs, sleeves, gloves. Also of the bones sleeved in flesh. Juices of the sunrise. Joins and veins of the same. Vermilion look of the hand held against a candle with the darker parts as the middles of the fingers and especially the knuckles covered with ash.
>
> From *Selected Works of Gerard Manley Hopkins*, (Gerard Manley Hopkins, Penguin)

To develop this skill in the classroom is relatively straightforward. A common focus is needed – perhaps something a little unusual, highly visual as a starting point. I have used the following with some success:

A candle
A mirror
Autumn leaves
Marbling
A stuffed owl
Slides of a spider
Pictures of magnified skin
Bark of a tree
Looking at hands with magnifying glasses
Flowers
Photos of snow
Glass bottles
Shells
A collection of shiny objects
Clocks
Storms
Snowfall

Teasels
Vegetables chopped in half
Visit to a deserted railway station.

The starting points you use will depend on what is to hand and to some extent on where you live. For instance, anyone living near the coast may use objects found on the beach or a view of a storm as a focus. Someone working in Gloucester may make use of the Cathedral windows, a burnt-out car or artefacts from the dock area.

Rapid brainstorming helps to generate possible ideas, words and phrases. Pupils should be used to jotting down ideas, trying a few similes, some alliteration perhaps. The essence of the poem will come through careful observation and rapidly listing words to describe – to re-create. This will mean looking carefully, noting details, using the senses. A class brainstorm, with pupils calling out ideas, can act as a useful strategy for generating ideas. It also provides an opportunity for the teacher to challenge the class, pushing for synonyms, pursuing possibilities as well as drawing them back to look more closely at the subject.

Look for the sorts of words that will bring the experience alive, avoiding abstract ideas and rooting the words in the concrete. For a flame one might well list words such as matches, rattle, shake, shiver, quiver, crack, hiss, flare, spit, leap, flame, red, orange, scarlet, flicker, flick, leap, dodge, dart, dive, lean, nudge, dither, fidget, sways, curls, shine, shimmer, gleam, glisten, glitter, glow, shadow, slip, slide, slither, crack, crackle, hiss, spit, and so forth. Looking at the pointed shape of the flame might elicit images such as tongue, peak, leaf, eye, mouth, wave, nail. These might be extended – a red eye stares in the dark. Often the words needed are of action and description. Try for a very long list – this technique of gathering words shows children how to look and notice, filtering words and ideas through the mind, rapidly responding to an experience.

Once pupils begin writing, such a list need not be stuck to too rigidly – more confident writers will take off on their own tack, weaker writers may be more dependent. The more experience young writers have of using this technique the swifter they can brainstorm for themselves. Brainstorming, at its best, bridges the gap between the abstract experience and the re-creation of that experience as a poem. It is linked to learning how to look at the truth of experience, how to name that experience, how to become a 'wordsearcher'.

Skeleton Leaf

Lifeless
Like tissue paper –
Frail animal bones.
A web of veins
Criss-crossing an old hand.
Map contours;
Dry streams.
I trace each tiny thread.
Dead lines.
Fine hairs woven
Into a lace lattice.

Sally, year 8

Tuning in the senses

Tuning young writers into using their senses and noticing detail lies at the root of all good writing. Rooting narrative and poetry into the tangible rather than the abstract will provide the basis for successful creative writing.

There are a number of good poems that can open up the opportunity to tune into the senses. Carol Ann Duffy opens her collection *The Oldest Girl in the World* (Faber 2000) with the title poem. In the poem the oldest girl in the world remembers her sense impressions from long ago. What other persona may be adopted to recall sense impressions in a similar way? In one class I worked with recently we agreed a short list of the following:

Gandalf
Oldest witch/wizard
Oldest boy/man/woman...
Rip Van Winkle
Sleeping Princess
Man in the Moon
Joseph
From an old people's home, they remember...

The success of the original poem lies partly in the way the poet selects a range of ideas. Duffy also manages to almost become different creatures (*I could taste like the fang of a snake*):

Children, I remember how I could hear
with my soft young ears
the tiny sounds of the air –
tinkles and chimes
like miniscule bells
ringing continually there;
clinks and chinks
like glasses of sparky gooseberry wine,
jolly and glinting and raised in the air.

Yes, I could hear like a bat. And how!
Can't hear a sniff of it now.
                    from *The Oldest Girl in the World*
                        by Carol Ann Duffy

James Berry's poem 'Childhood Tracks' from
Playing a Dazzler (Puffin 1996) is rooted in his
childhood memories:

Eating crisp fried fish with plain bread.
Eating sheared ice made into 'snowball'
With syrup in a glass.
Eating young jelly-coconut, mixed
With village-made wet sugar.
Drinking cool water from a calabash gourd
On worked land in the hills.
                    From *Childhood Tracks* by James Berry

This can be a successful approach for recalling
sense impressions from childhood – especially for
children who have lived in other countries or have
strong memories of holidays. Brainstorming, or
listing ideas under headings for each sense, may
be a useful tactic. I often add in a section about
memories. 'Memory Senses' (on p. 25) is my own
simple version – a memory sense collection.

List poems

One of the simplest ways into poetry is through
listing. The Japanese poet Sei Shonaghan used this
technique and wrote a whole book of lists (e.g. List of
shiny things, list of soft things). Just looking around
the room I am working in gives me the following.

List of white things

The walls reflecting the snow outside.
Two candles balanced on a shelf.
Cushions scattered on the sofa.
Pages in a well-thumbed book.
The edge of a painting.
Words on a blue background.
Patterns woven into the carpet.

Gary Snyder wrote a poem titled 'Things to do around
a Lookout'. This is literally a list of things that can be
done while hanging around. When I run writing days
in schools this can act as a quick warm-up,
introducing me to the area and the group's interests.

Things to do Around Hastings

Mooch around the old town staring into shops.
Hang about on the pier –
Watch the fishermen throw sandwiches
Out to the gulls.
Listen to the ice cream vans yodelling.

Watch old people sitting on the front
Just staring at the empty sea.
Try to spot France across the Channel.
Watch the French students trailing
Round the so called sights.
Dodge the waves smashing
Over the promenade
On a stormy day.

The secret of making a list poem interesting is
twofold:

● select your items to go into the list with care –
  make them differ, offer contrasts and surprises;
● try to make each item special in some way –
  perhaps by using the words you choose in a
  surprising way.

Morning/night – starless and bible-black

Key times of the day. I have used the opening of
'Under Milk Wood' read by Richard Burton as a way
into writing about dawn creeping across a village/
town/city. There is something about the rhythm of
the language and the richness of his voice that
catches many children's imaginations. Sometimes
this leads to rather fanciful writing, where suddenly
the streets of Pimlico become paved with cobbles!

Another way in is to create a 'praise poem',
thanking, blessing or welcoming different things
that are happening merely for their occurrence.
Some sort of repetitive structure may enable this
or just an opening line to introduce a list. A pair of
complementary poems that would fit in well with
this session are 'For Francesca' and 'Small Dawn
Song' by the Bristol poets Helen Dunmore and
Philip Gross, both found in *The Apple Raid*, edited
by Pie Corbett (Macmillan 2001).

With the class, make a list of sights, sounds,
smells, tastes associated with dawn. Use some sort
of repeating phrase to link these, for example:

Thank you
To the blackbird dithering in the hedge,
To the lone bus trundling up the street,
To the postman slipping letters
Into the doors' slim mouths…

Thank you
To the kettle burbling in the corner,
The toast smouldering,
The slick spread of marmalade,
The bite of coffee.

Memory Senses

I like to watch
my cat stalk along the wall
then slip, slim as a wish,
beneath the gate.
I like to watch
the stars freckle the dark,
the thin moon's grin,
and the city lights strung out
like fiery beads.
I like to watch
the belisha beacon blink
its orange eye,
the black taxis beetling
down back alleys,
and the sudden rain
goose pimpling the road.

Ears and eyes.
Nose and tongue -
with skin I prize
my world.

I like to listen to the sound
of the t.v. mumbling downstairs
as the night lengthens,
the last bell at the end of the day,
and the scrunch of paper unwrapping,
I like to listen
to the distant siren wobbling,
chattering at the Saturday market stalls
and the deep warmth
of my father's voice.

Ears and eyes.
Nose and tongue -
with skin I prize
my world.

I like the smell of
the salty sea wind in Cornwall,
bacon hissing and spitting in the frying
   pan,
and chocolate mixed for a cake,

Ears and eyes.
Nose and tongue -
with skin I prize
my world.

I like the taste of
salty chips on a cold winter's night,
the bitter taste of too much vinegar
that made my tongue curl,
and the sweet bite of ice cream,
so cold that teeth ache.
I like the taste of
of an apple slice
and the sudden fizz of cola
as it bursts in your mouth.

I like to touch
the warm, smooth fur
as my cat makes an arch
of her silky back,
and the cool skin
of a wet glass of milk
on a hot day.

I like to remember
The close earth,
The underside of leaves,
The parachute of trees' branches
Spread above me.
Each bright day,
Sharp as lemon,
True as salt
Sizzling on my tongue.

Pie Corbett

Dawn Song

It's still dark –
A hint of light
Hits the horizon.

A scatter of bright stars
Pinprick the velvet dark.

The moon is nowhere
To be seen.

Dew clings to the grass.

Spiders' webs decorate
The rose bushes.

The birds are up –
Punctuating the dawn
With a few frail notes.

From the doorway
I watch the cat
Bound across the lawn.

Steam rises from my tea –
The dream slips away
From my mind.

The cold brings me back inside
As the central heating kicks in.

Pie Corbett

In my poem 'Dawn Song' (on p. 26) I have taken a more descriptive tack. It is simply a list of descriptive points. You could use this to set the scene – to sharpen the language.

Poems of solitary delights

So much of the poetry that young writers write in key stage 3/4 is built around exploring their own confusions and often negative feelings. Tachibana Akemi's 'Poems of Solitary Delights' (on p. 28) offer a simple way to remind ourselves of what we like, to celebrate the small miracles of life.

Read the poems through; which do the class prefer? Why? Make a list of small things that give pleasure. Just off the top of my head I jotted down:

A cool pillow, Smelling a new book, The fizz of lemonade on my tongue, Feeling better after flu, Watching a fly clean its legs, When my aunt says she is going, Doodling in the margin, The smell of bacon, Slicing cucumber, Watching snowflakes, A bus finally arriving, The opening of a film

Look carefully at the form of the poem, especially the use of commas to bracket off a subordinate clause. Demonstrate how to imitate the structure, for example:

*What a delight it is
When, after two hours
Of listening to recipes,
My aunt puts on her hat
And leaves us alone.*

*What a delight it is
When, feeling lonely,
I am joined by a fly
That carefully cleans
Its spindly legs.*

Notice that each mini poem starts in the same way, has five lines and drops in a clause. Probably the hardest part of the session is to prompt the class to think about things they enjoy! It can help to ask them to think about the smallest pleasures. I used to enjoy twanging my ruler – and have always sworn that it is a useful tactic when stuck for ideas!

*What a delight it is
When, stuck for the next
Line in a poem,
I twang my ruler and listen
To the energy hum.*

Ways of looking

Observation is one way of looking – but there are other ways to see and represent the world. Wallace Stevens' poem 'Thirteen Ways of Looking at a Blackbird' has acted as a springboard for many writers creating their own mini poems about one subject. As with list poems of any sort the skill is in finding different ways to 'look' at the subject.

1   *Among twenty snowy mountains
    The only moving thing
    Was the eye of the blackbird.*

2   *I was of three minds,
    Like a tree
    In which there are three blackbirds.*
        Wallace Stevens, from 'Thirteen Ways of
    Looking at a Blackbird', *The Collected Poems of
    Wallace Stevens*, Faber, 1955

A prompt list of possible strategies for varying each idea might be useful for some classes. In other words, each numbered verse could take a different standpoint (see page 29 for an example).

Wishes
Descriptions
Instructions
Newspaper headlines
Jokes
Riddles
Inventions
Memories
Conversations
Questions
Exclamations
Dreams

Another approach is to remind young writers of possible techniques. Each idea could be made special by using a different technique (see page 30). To vary each verse you could try:

Simile using 'like'
Simile using 'as'
Extended metaphor
Personification
Alliteration
Onomatopoeia
Rhyme

A final tactic is to think about different approaches (see page 31).

Make the subject speak:

Exaggerate or boast, Compare, Talk to the subject, Create an opposite, Contradict the subject, Tell a lie about it. You could also:

Transform the subject, Muddle the senses, Offer advice, Reveal a secret, Say something new.

Poems of Solitary Delights

What a delight it is
When on the bamboo matting
In my grass-thatched hut,
All on my own
I make myself at ease.

What a delight it is
When, borrowing
Rare writings from a friend,
I open out
The first sheet.

What a delight it is
When, spreading paper,
I take my brush
And find my hand
Better than I thought.

What a delight it is
When, after a hundred days
Of racking my brains,
That verse that wouldn't come
Suddenly turns out well.

What a delight it is
When, of a morning,
I get up and go out
To find in full bloom a flower
That yesterday was not there.

Tachibana Akemi

From *The Penguin Book of Japanese Verse*, translated by Bownas and Thwaite (Penguin, 1966)

Six Ways of Looking at a Gate

1 The gate wishes
   that the wind
   would leave off
   tugging
   at its elbow.

2 The gate sports a new coat
   of timber wood varnish.

3 Gate – get shut!

4 Gate in multi-million post scandal!

5 What is the difference between a gate and a
   goat?
   (If you don't know the answer to that one then
   give up the idea of becoming a postman.)

6 What stops entry
   and protects?
   Yes – it's a gate, folks!

Key

1 Wishes
2 Descriptions
3 Instructions
4 Newspaper headlines
5 Jokes
6 Riddles

Pie Corbett

Six Ways of Looking at a Lemon

1 It sits in the bowl
   like a cold yellow
   planet.

2 On the tongue
   it is sharp
   as a cat's bite.

3 A still heart,
   grown cold,
   plucked from the chest
   of a restless man.

4 OK, so the lemon
   winked at me.

5 The luminous lemon
   lies lazily
   in a languid lagoon of light.

Key

1 Simile using 'like'
2 Simile using 'as'
3 Extended metaphor
4 Personification
5 Alliteration

Pie Corbett

Six Ways of Looking at EastEnders

1   'Watcha lookin' at,
    me ole china?'

2   I am by far and away
    the best looking,
    coolest, sweetest,
    most popular programme –
    ever.

3   EastEnders is like
    a smack on the back
    of the head.

4   Why are you
    always messing about
    with other people's lives.
    Hands off!

5   EastEnders – Noddy!

6   It can only be seen
    on the white bellies
    of clouds.

Key

1   Make the subject speak
2   Exaggerate or boast
3   Compare
4   Talk to the subject
5   Create an opposite
6   Tell a lie about it

Pie Corbett

Autobiography

Teaching Focus

To use memory and everyday experience as a source for poetry; to experiment with making everyday experience memorable; to experiment with rhyme and rhythm.

Of course, our own life, real and imagined, is the source of all that we write. Valuing, exploring, celebrating our own autobiography can become a satisfying project as it celebrates who we are. Memory is a vital source for all writers, and indeed, most of what is written as narrative is based upon the amalgamation of memory.

I first came across this approach through reading Adrian Henri's *Autobiography*. If this is not to hand, then begin by looking at the example provided on page 36. Notice how it is structured and discuss the different memories. Already some of these mini poems may prompt the class to think of their own ideas. These should be noted down immediately before they are forgotten. Share your own anecdotes, as these will also prompt other memories. Everybody should be building up a list of possible ideas.

Some time needs to be spent in listing possible memories for inclusion. It may help to begin by listing key events in chronological order. Then between these events begin to add in memories. It helps to spend a session sharing anecdotes, as one anecdote will help prompt other ideas. It is worth pointing out from the beginning that large and dramatic memories are not necessary – small details may be all that is needed to bring back a time, event or place.

This prompt list may help to trigger some ideas:

Moving home
Changing schools
Friends
Sad times
Fear
Holiday places
Secret places
Celebrations
Tricks
Funny things
The most important event in my life

Strange relatives
Trying not to cry
A lie
Jealousy
What makes me angry

It can help if members of the class bring in old photographs, interview those at home about early experiences, use letters, old diaries and so forth. Many of us keep special objects in our bedrooms – a stone from a beach, a wooden box, a memento from a holiday. These could also appear in the poem so that it becomes a collage of our lives – places we have been, people met, things seen and done. Drawing out a time line can help to prompt a sequence of mini poems.

The actual style of the poem echoes the free approach of Adrian Henri's original and many children find this style liberating. It is an interesting mixture of poetry and prose.

The idea of turning our lives into a series of sections, then under each section numbering a range of mini memories, can be a helpful way to structure our past. This list can be added to over time.

Anecdotes

Michael Rosen paved the way for the anecdotal poem. Much of his writing is based on his memories of school days or his own family life. They are mainly crafted anecdotes. The best have that ring of truth that echoes with all of us – a good example is his poem about car journeys, with the constant refrain of 'are we nearly there' and Mum threatening to leave the children by the side of the road! He manages to pinpoint personal experiences that touch a common chord.

This sort of session needs to begin with a trawl back through possible anecdotes. A prompt list of ideas can be handy. I usually read out the list and then tell a few anecdotes myself. They do not have to be funny or sad – just moments we remember will do. After all, if you remembered it then it must have some significance.

Prompts for anecdotes

A row at home.
In trouble at school.

Hospital visit.
Moving home.
New school.
Old relatives.
A wedding.
Sad times.
Pets.
First day at school.
Odd people.
A frightening place.
April fools' day.
Birthday treats.
What makes people at home mad.
Embarrassing moment.
Lying/stealing/sneaking.
Gossip.

It helps for the class to tell their anecdotes in pairs. They should be aware of the need to choose something that is sufficiently focused and self-contained or else the writing will become too lengthy and weighty. One clear idea is enough. The writing needs to emulate the anecdotal style, choosing line breaks at sensible points. (See poem on page 37.)

'The Red Wheelbarrow'/ 'This is Just to Say'

There is something about these two poems (on pages 38 and 39). I cannot quite put my finger on it but just about everyone who writes hold these little gems in high regard. They mingle everyday experience and language in a particular manner.

'The Red Wheelbarrow'

'The Red Wheelbarrow' has a simple enough pattern (pairs of lines with three words/one word). Notice how the line ends drop down the meaning – wheel/barrow, rain/water, white/chickens. The contrast of colours – red/white. The power of the word 'glazed' – almost as if the poem is a painting, varnished.

The poem focuses upon the barrow: what is happening, where it is. It is a three-part movement.

The simplicity of the picture is reminiscent of a haiku or a 'poem of solitary delight'. It reminds me of the black and white photos of Henri Cartier-Bresson.

Then there is the whole question of the opening lines, 'so much depends upon'. What on earth does that mean? After all, the likelihood is

that nothing depends on this at all. But as writers we have been giving significance to our lives, our memories, our imaginings, celebrating even the slightest detail.

What else might be given such status? Perhaps this is a case for taking the familiar and making it special. Choosing the insignificant and carefully crafting, selecting, sifting to the barest of bones without becoming 'over-poetic' or fancifying the language – one well-chosen image and a powerful verb should do the trick. Spend some time listing possible ideas. From where I am sitting several options spring to mind just by looking around the room and out of the window (and a memory just popped itself in as I was typing – a strong image from my childhood):

Church spire
Shadow of a glass
Brass door handle
Cracks in the ceiling

Try demonstrating an idea, talking through your thinking. For instance:

Common start	*So much depends upon*
The object plus colour	*The grey church spire*
What is happening/ description	*Trimmed with snow flakes*
Where it is plus colour	*By the green pines*

Having just written the above I met two problems. I tried to be faithful to the original pattern. If you decide to follow the pattern strictly then selecting a pair of words to drop down as line breaks needs thought – church/spire, snow/flakes. In the last part I wanted 'in front of' but it gave me too many words.

Now I will try the same process without worrying so much about following the pattern in any set way – but using the writing just to celebrate.

So much depends
upon

The wine glass's
shadow

trembling as I
write

against the white
wall.

That was easier. I'll try one more:

> So much depends
> upon
>
> The dark crack
> in the plaster
>
> Like a spidery ink
> track
>
> Traced across a white
> ceiling.

Well, a free interpretation is easier to play with. Perhaps the best advice is to attempt several of these mini poems, experimenting as you go. Focus on naming the object, describing it and placing it. I found the idea of contrasting colours helpful too.

'This is Just to Say'

This poem is equally striking. I love the way the title shifts into the poem. Students will pick up on the cheekiness of the message. Is he really sorry for having eaten the plums? What sorts of things have you done that you were not really sorry for? It may be worth making a collective list of possible ideas. I usually share the following that will strike a chord with most students:

This is Just to Say

> I have not
> bothered
> to complete
> the home
> work that
> you set
> last week
> and you
> were so
> insistent
> about.
>
> Forgive me,
> last night's
> film
> was so
> exciting.

Messages for mice

One class I worked with had great fun with messages. This all started at about the time of the televised version of *The Borrowers*. My children were quite young and they had cottoned on to the idea that there might be small people living in the house. Daisy, who must have been about three years old at the time, swore blind that she had seen a Borrower in her room. That started the ball rolling. The next thing we knew there were sightings throughout the house, in the garden and anywhere we travelled. They acquired names and histories – whole families sprang up.

Then I was tempted into writing a letter from a Borrower and leaving it out at night, to be found in the morning. This started a lengthy correspondence. The children wrote letters and did drawings and the Borrowers replied. Poppy was at school and her friends also began to write. The letters and messages had to be left by Borrower holes – in the kitchen, by the back door, at the end of the garden. The correspondence escalated. In the end I had to send all the Borrowers on a summer holiday to the fields. They made a brief reappearance that Christmas but since then have been on extended leave!

Well, I told this class about what was happening and we decided that it might be interesting to write messages for different animals. I wrote a few – a note for the cat, the dog, a mosquito – and then for a nightmare (see poems on pages 40–41).

I began to find messages creeping into unlikely places. My mark book received several curt notes, messages arrived for the red pen, and the Corbett tie collection received a number of severe warnings about excesses!

Looking back, this idea would build well on the William Carlos Williams poem 'This is Just to Say'. It knocks further at the question, 'What is a Poem?' I am not sure that it matters. I am more interested in young writers imaginatively playing with their world and their language. And we had some fun. Dirty word probably, and I have yet to see an objective that stated 'Enjoy playing with language and ideas'. Go on, treat yourself: slip it into your schemes of work. Who knows – the next Ofsted Inspector might approve of the idea that an objective may be to find pleasure in handling language. Only a madman would disagree. (Do quote me.)

Fine-tuning everyday speech

If autobiography, everyday life, can become the stuff of poetry, then so too can everyday speech. A number of writers work in the area of performance poetry that makes direct use of everyday language. Ian McMillan talks about this sort of poetry as 'fine-tuning everyday speech'. It does help if you have an ear for the rhythms of speech – or you can take a phrase and say it in a sing-song, rhythmic manner. For instance, on my travels around the country I have become familiar with the names of lorry firms and those which mend our roads – Norbert Dentressangle and Eddie Stobart to pick on two. Take the name 'Eddie Stobart' and chant it rhythmically:

Edd-ie Sto-bart
Edd-ie Sto-bart

Then extend the rhythm, chucking in a rhyme, for example:

Edd-ie Sto-bart
Edd-ie Sto-bart
He got going
On a go-cart.

It can be easy enough to construct whole poems like this. A repeated chorus may help the rhyme to jingle along. Selecting a theme that everyone knows about can provide a useful focus. For instance, everyone eats:

Bangers and mash
Bangers and mash
Makes your stomach
Bang and crash

Beans on toast
Beans on toast
Open wide
And past the post.

Keep the verses going and then invent a chorus about food, for example:

Down the hatch –
Open wide
Let that grub
Slip and slide.

Names can offer another way into writing in this vein. (This is where a rhyming dictionary can be very useful.) Years ago I taught a girl called Melissa Dare. The name seemed to me to have a rhythmic beat (perhaps I had to say that name so many times that it took on a life of its own!).

Melissa Dare
Melissa Dare
I see her here
And everywhere.

What's she done, where's she been?
Melissa Dare wasn't seen –

On the train track
Down the town
In the pool
For half a crown

At the seaside
Watching telly
Get a suntan
On your belly.

This sort of writing can be a little wacky, with the rhythm and the rhymes leading the verses. It is all part of the liberating effect of attacking rhythm. Another way in is to begin with a word that appeals and take it further. Brian Moses has a wonderful slapstick poem in this vein about a jellyfish that starts with the word 'jellyfish'. It begins:

Jellyfish, jellyfish
Floats along and slaps you on the belly fish.

Just when you thought you'd go for a swim,
Just when you thought it was safe to go in.

Jelllyfish, jellyfish,
Saw one in a programme on the telly fish.

Thinking about it kept me awake,
I just don't think that I can take

Jellyfish, jellyfish,
Trod on one at Margate with Aunt Nelly fish.

Brian Moses, from Hippopotamus Dancing,
(Cambridge 1994)

Perhaps a way into this would be to begin by brainstorming favourite words and then selecting one that has plenty of other words that rhyme with it. Let us take a word like 'Runner bean' and see what can be done.

Runner bean
Runner bean
Makes a logo
For designer jeans.

Runner bean
Runner bean
Served up daily
To the Queen

You can eat them hot
You can eat them cool
You can serve them up
By the swimming pool.

Not earth-shattering stuff I know. But this sort of rhythmic dash can help to loosen up the bonds, make children feel that they can contribute, that their own language can make poetry, their words can sing. And when performed by a group with vigour, using clapping and stamping as a background, it sounds good. Experiment with different patterns and rhythms.

Autobiography – Part 1

1   Standing in the playground
at my first school – quite lost.
So many big children – not knowing what to do or where to go.

2   Assembly.
Sitting on the shiny wooden floor staring at the cracks.
Singing hymns and having to mouth the words aloud.
Watching clouds drift by the jam jars on the classroom window.
Bringing in a bunch of daffodils, the stems crunched together.
Watching tadpoles spin round in the class goldfish bowl.
Filling my best friend Petie's wellington boots with tadpoles.

3   Falling off the back of a truck.
Feeling my leg snap and waiting, twisted on the ground
while the van backs towards me, over me.
Smelling the darkness beneath the van's breath
as my friends screamed.

4   Moving from the village.
To our new house.
It smelt strange.
Sunlight waking me every morning.
My cat found one winter in the snow,
curled asleep like a question mark.

5   Arriving at the big school.
How many reasons can you find for not doing homework?
Petie fell ill.
In hospital, still as a baby,
On a life support machine.
I watched his face and prayed his life back again.

6   Holidays
at the sands – waves wrinkling the sea.
Walking with no shoes on.
Latenight fish and chips, salt and vinegar tang.
Dad laughing – remembering his laugh
that is now silent.

Pie Corbett

Diary poem – Snake

A sunny afternoon
round by the garage, chatting to Ted –
my eye caught sight
of something moving –
a snake zigzagging across the road,
like a dark, thick rope.
Its head raised and held back,
hissing as it sneaked its way
towards the grass.
Ted rushed to the van
and got his camera,
took several shots,
down close to its head.
The snake paused,
posed, head held back
as if to strike.
Body tensed in each coil,
hissing.
Its tiny black eyes
fixed on Ted's hands.

Then we let it go
up into the grass beyond
the war memorial –
we lost it there, where
the grass gets longer –
we couldn't see it any more
or even feel the grass shaking,
the snake making its way
intent upon its own business.

Pie Corbett

The Red Wheelbarrow

so much depends
upon

a red wheel
barrow

glazed with rain
water

beside the white
chickens

William Carlos Williams

From The Collected Poems of William Carlos Williams, © Carcanet Press Ltd, in
The Penguin Book of American Verse (Penguin)

This is Just to Say

I have eaten
the plums
that were in
the icebox

and which
you were probably
saving for breakfast

Forgive me
they were delicious
so sweet
and so cold

William Carlos Williams

From The Collected Poems of William Carlos Williams, © Carcanet Press Ltd, in
The Penguin Book of American Verse (Penguin)

Message for the Mice that Live in the Roof

I've left you a present.

It's all I could find –

just a chunk of sweaty cheddar

that had gone hard,

and some cold bacon rind.

Sorry but –

there was nothing classier

in the fridge,

and I didn't think

that you'd care

for scraps of garlic.

(I've left the cheese

on the red dish

by the cat

flap.)

Pie Corbett

Message for the Mosquito who Shares my Bedroom

I'm fed up
with the way
you keep me awake.

You wait
till I've just turned the light off
and settled down
for a good night's zizzzzz
before starting up
your irritating whine,
announcing,
'Mister Mosquito
is out for a bit.'

At any second
I expect to feel you
puncture my skin
and suck my blood.

Tiny vampire,
I am not your personal
Ketchup bottle.
If I find you've settled nearby,
I'll swat you flat.
Be warned –
go pester
some other sauce
of blood.

Pie Corbett

Monologues and Other Voices

Carol Anne Duffy has mined the area of monologues most successfully and many of her poems in *The World's Wife* are worth sharing with pupils (though some are too steamy!). In 'The Wolf's Wife Speaks' (see page 45) I have included a monologue spoken by 'the wolf's wife' from the fairy-tale 'The Three Little Pigs'.

It is worth making a list of possible characters – those who are mentioned in nursery rhymes, fairy-tales, myths or legends that might lend themselves to written monologues. Characters who make a minor appearance or who do not appear but might be relations are useful too.

To write the poem, the writer has to be familiar with the original tale. Do not discount the idea of a speedy rereading of 'Little Red Riding Hood', for instance. Then list possible characters who might become the voice of the poem – Red's mother, father, brother, sister, teacher, the woodcutter's relatives, grandpa (they got divorced and he lives in a semi in Budleigh Salterton).

Role-play may offer a way into the poem. This can be carried out in pairs with one character in role as a neighbour and the other adopting the main role. The neighbour just has to listen. The main character talks about what has happened, offering comments, judgements, gossip and possibly a nod to the future. The anecdotal style would build well upon anecdotal poems (see page 32).

Meetings with midnight

Both of Carol Anne Duffy's collections for young readers seem to me to provide sufficient meat for young writers to use as a springboard. One of my favourites is her poem 'Meeting Midnight' (see page 48). This is a strange monologue in which the poem's voice talks about a meeting with midnight. The idea reminded me of the fantasy stories of Tanith Lee or of Diana Wynne Jones – both rich, meaty writers of fantasy.

The poem calls upon the Cinderella tale, using some ideas based in reality (her eyes were sparkling pavements after frost) and others where the imagination has taken a leap (she smoked a small cheroot). Rhyme is occasionally used, where it provides a jump forward that enriches the poem.

Who else might we meet? A quick brainstorm with a group of young writers in Bristol provided the following ideas:

Night, Dawn, Midday, Dusk, Evening, Nightfall.

Then we took the idea further:

Bird-song, Death, Life, Hope, War, Jealousy, Anger, Pain, Joy, Future, Past, Eternity, Silence, Confusion, Winter, Frost, Thunder, Snow, The Moon, The Sun.

We selected two different ideas to work on as a class – 'Dusk' and 'Pain' – and began by brainstorming ideas for each. I prompted thought by asking: What does it look like? What is it made of? Where does it go? Who might it meet? What happens? See the first drafts of 'Dusk' and 'Pain' on pages 46 and 47. These could be used to practise revising.

Green bears

The idea of transformation into a totally new and different creature is an appealing one. Kafka's *Metamorphosis* might set the scene for this idea – or perhaps contrasting the opening of this with the opening of Anne Fine's 'Bill's New Frock', a story that many young writers will know. It is the same notion – you have become a changeling.

One of the most playful aspects of poetry is to name things – and then rename. Poems can re-create our vision of the world or create a new order. Richard Edwards wrote a poem which starts with the words, 'I am a green bear'. It is another monologue, spoken by an invented creature. I am fairly certain that he in turn had been reading Kenneth Patchen's poem 'The Magical Mouse' which begins in a similar vein: 'I am the magical Mouse'.

Both poems use similar tactics to structure the ideas:

- occasional repetition of the opening line (e.g. 'I am a green bear');
- mentioning what I do not do and then what I do (e.g. 'I don't eat cheese/I eat sunsets/and the tops of trees');
- mentioning what I eat, what I fear (or don't fear), where I live, how I sound, my colour.

Both poems use powerful imagery. Patchen's ends: 'I eat/Little birds – and maidens/That taste like dust'.

What creature would you like to be? How could you make this animal totally new? I have always thought that relying on using the word 'magical' is a cop-out, so another way of making the creature new is needed. Using a colour is a potent idea and can lead on to other possibilities for the poem. For instance, with one class we decided to focus on the possibility of creating a red wolf. We began by brainstorming ideas associated with the word red:

Sunsets, Dawn, Flames, Post-boxes, London buses, Exercise books, Blood, Wine, Traffic-lights.

We then tried to make each idea more specific – to add in that extra layer of detail or mystery:

A scarlet sunset over Timbuctoo, Dawn on the South Downs, A candle flame from a wedding, A Post-box full of wishes, A London bus travelling nowhere, An exercise book complete with the history of the universe, Christ's last drop of blood, A sip of red wine stolen from the lips of a lady, Traffic-lights at stop.

We then made a list of possible sentence starters to provide some prompts:

I taste...
I grab...
I look at...
I smell...
I listen to...
At night.... In the morning....

See my draft of 'The Red Wolf' on page 49 for class comment.

An owl inside of me

Carl Sandburg's poem 'Wilderness' acts as an invitation to explore the territories of the body and the soul. In it he seems to speak as if he was the wilderness and lists the creatures that roam within his lands.

There is a wolf in me.... Fangs pointed for tearing gashes...
There is a hog in me.... A snout and a belly...

I have often used this idea playfully to list all the creatures that roam within the wilderness of our selves. What sorts of creatures do you like? If you had to be an animal what would you choose? After reading Philip Pullman's wonderful *Northern Lights* trilogy (*His Dark Materials*) my family had some good discussions in this vein – if you had a 'daemon' or 'familiar' what form would this take? Reggie Perrin saw his mother-in-law as a hippo. How do you see your friends and family?

This can make a whole poem or act as a playful warm up. Model an example, perhaps sticking to couplets about favourite creatures that you feel an affinity with, for example:

There is an owl inside of me
Whose amber eye is fixed on the world.

There is a lizard inside of me
Soaking in the sun, tongue flickering.

Brian Patten's poem 'Tiger Shadows' (see page 50) provides a more challenging focus, extending the metaphor. It would be worth exploring some of the patterns used that might be helpful in one's own version, underlining useful words or phrases, for example:

I wish I was...
I'd...
While..., I'd...
If I were a... my eyes..., my tail..., etc.
I would discover...
I would...

It can help to add in other possibilities, for example:

I'd listen to
I'd touch
I'd taste
I sniff
I'd wait for
I'd wander, etc.

A useful way into this is to brainstorm what is known about the creature – what it looks like, what it does, where it lives, its habits – links with known stories, etc. Some of this information may be useful and act as prompts for writing ideas.

Cat Began

Andrew Matthews' poem 'Cat Began' (see page 51) seems to provide yet another way into using poetry to transform – to create a creature from the scraps of the world. It is a simple enough idea. What is needed to create the cat's voice, coat, walk, eyes and claws? The pattern can be emulated so that less confident students may lean heavily upon the original. More confident writers will take the principle but create their own structures.

Of course, creating different creatures will mean looking at different parts of the chosen subject. An elephant will need a thick skin, tusks, a short tail, large feet, a mighty weight, trunk, and a long memory to boot!

Draw attention to the way in which Andrew Matthews describes 'the howling of the wind . . . the screeching of the owl . . . the softness of the snow', etc. This structure will help the less confident and may need demonstrating in a class version.

Wolf began.
He grabbed the grating of steel,
He stole the soul of the wind,
He grasped the screams from a torturer's past
And created his voice.

For his coat
He took the grey of cold ashes from a burnt out
*   village,*
He took a handful of dust from the roadside to hell,
He took the smoothness from a baby's cheek.

The Wolf's Wife Speaks

He was always out and about.
first on the block
to be up at the crack of dawn
sniffing the morning air.

Of course,
pork was his favourite.
I tell you, he would go a long way
for a nice bit of crackling,
or to catch a tasty piglet or two.

But in the end
it all got too much –
all that huffing and puffing
up and down the den,
muttering in his sleep
that he would blow the house
    down!

Something was wrong,
I could tell –
some thing had put his nose
out of joint.

He'd come home full of bravado,
swaggering into the den,
flashing me that wolfish grin –
all teeth and tongue –
then he'd set about boasting,
full of big talk about
blowing up another building.
it cut no ice with me.

The tell-tale signs were there -
some days he'd get back
covered in straw,
hardly able to draw breath.

What he'd been up to,
Lord alone knows . . . .

Well, it all came to a head,
when late one afternoon –
he shot back in,
with his fur singed.

I had to laugh –
he looked so funny,
stood there with his bare bottom
red as a radish.
Talk about coming home
with his tail between his legs!
Where he'd been – I can't
    imagine.
He never said.

He stays more at home now.
Well, he's prone to bronchitis –
this time of year you can hear him
    coming,
poor old thing –
wheezing and puffing,
hardly able to draw breath.

We don't talk about it –
and he's right off pork!
If you ask me,
it's all been
a bit of a blow
to his ego.

Pie Corbett

Dusk *(first draft)*

I met Dusk.

His hands trembled with shadows.

He wore a coat of cobwebs, grey as smoke.

His hat was tugged right down

And I could only just see

The dark stain on his lips.

He strode through the city streets

With me running, running

On his heels

Like a lap dog.

I saw him meet night.

Night stretched out and touched dusk.

He faded fast.

At last I was alone.

Except for the darkness

That clung like a cloak.

No joke!

Pie Corbett

Pain (first draft)

I met Pain.

She was highly strung.

Wringing her hands

Like a mangle.

Her eyes twisted like a spiral.

And that heart!

Why it beat so loud

That I could see its red pulse.

She left behind her a trail

Of frozen puddles,

A scattering of broken mirrors –

Endless bad luck.

She met her ending.

Gratefully, she melted.

But her end

Was also

A beginning.

Pain –

Is so thinning.

Pie Corbett

Meeting Midnight

I met Midnight.
Her eyes were sparkling pavements after frost.
She wore a full-length, dark-blue raincoat with a
    hood.
She winked. She smoked a small cheroot.

I followed her.
Her walk was more a shuffle, more a dance.
She took the path to the river, down she went.
On Midnight's scent,
I heard the twelve cool syllables, her name,
chime from the town.
When those bells stopped,

Midnight paused by the water's edge.
She waited there.
I saw a girl in purple on the bridge.
It was One o'Clock.
Hurry, Midnight said. *It's late, it's late.*
I saw them run together.
Midnight wept.
They kissed full on the lips.
and then I slept.

The next day I bumped into Half-Past Four.
He was a bore.

Carol Ann Duffy

From *Meeting Midnight* (Faber 1999)

The Red Wolf

I am the red wolf.

I don't eat rabbits
or snaffle young deer.
I eat candle flames
stolen from a wedding,
the red flickering
against a lacy white.

I am the red wolf.

I don't waste time
sniffing the scent of my next meal.
I smell the frost like sparks
from an iron furnace.

I am the red wolf.

I listen to your lips
sip red wine snatched
from the open mouths
of scoundrels.

I don't watch the pack
but stare at post-boxes
full of empty wishes
and traffic-lights held at Stop.

At night I dream
of an exercise book
complete with my history
and I wonder –
are there others out there,
red and memorable
as the last drop of blood
on a crown of horns?

Pie Corbett

Tiger Shadows

I wish I was a tiger in the Indian jungle
The jungle would be my teacher

No school
And the night sky a blackboard smudged with stars
I wish I was a tiger in the Indian jungle

Kitten-curious
I'd pad about on paws big as frying pans

While the monkeys chatted in the trees above me
I'd sniff the damp jungly air
Out of exotic flowers I would make a crown of pollen

If I were a tiger in the Indian jungle
My eyes would glitter among the dark green leaves
My tail would twitch like a snake

I would discover abandoned cities
Where no human feet had trod for centuries

I would be lord of a lost civilization
And leap among the vine-covered ruins

I wish I was a tiger in the Indian jungle
As the evening fell
I'd hum quiet tiger-tunes to which the fireflies would dance

I'd watch the red, bubbling sun
Go fishing with its net of shadows

While the hunters looked for me miles and miles away
I'd lie stretched out in my secret den

I would doze in the strawberry-coloured light
Under the golden stripy shadows of the trees
I would dream a tiger's dream

Brian Patten

From *Juggling with Gerbils* (Puffin 2000)

Cat Began

Cat began.
She took the howling of the wind,
She took the screeching of the owl
And made her voice.

For her coat
She took the softness of the snow,
She took the yellow of the sand,
She took the shadows of the branches of the trees.

From deep wells
She took the silences of stones,
She took the moving of the water
For her walk.

Then at night
Cat took the glittering of stars,
She took the blackness of the sky
To make her eyes.

Fire and ice
Went in the sharpness of her claws
And for their shape
She took the new moon's slender curve –

And Cat was made.

Andrew Matthews

From *Paws and Claws* (Hutchinson Children's Books 1995)

Deceptions and Wordplay

Teaching Focus

To experiment with metaphor and word play, using language and form creatively; to experiment with alliteration, imagery and surprising word combinations.

Telling lies

A lot of poetry is built around lies. 'My Love is like a red, red rose.' Absolute nonsense; she's nothing like a rose!

Of course lying in the everyday world is about deceiving people. If I say, 'I gave your mother the bunch of keys' when I did not, that is a lie designed to throw the tracker dogs off the scent. If I say, 'I gave your mother the bunch of smiles', that is also a lie. However, it is not meant to deceive but to illuminate. It is designed to communicate a different form of truth to the conventional everyday kind – a truth to do with the punch of an emotion.

As human beings we reach for this special form of language especially when emotion is involved. We use it when we are excited, moved, saddened, amazed and want to communicate what happened, what we saw and what we felt. Everyday language set out in everyday ways will not do – so we shift into using similes, metaphors, heightening the language, tuning it up. This seems to be quite natural. You only have to stand around on the 5th of November watching a firework display. The ooohs and aaahs are soon followed by 'they look like stars'. The caretaker from my last school, not a man given to poetic utterance, had woken one morning to find frost on the inside of his window. 'It was like a flame,' he muttered. There was pause. 'No, a fern, a feather, creeping up the window.' There you have it. Something unusual that could not be explained in ordinary ways and he found himself quite naturally reaching for poetic language.

In poetry this special form of lying is about transforming the world and illuminating it – looking at things in different ways to add in extra layers of perception. Looked at like this we have the strangest position – where the truth of an experience can sometimes be more strongly communicated by writing in a way that is false.

Poems are full of lies – images, metaphors, stories, striking contrasts, connections and comparisons – that, if read as everyday language, are often nonsense. If read as poetry, they may strike an echo of a new truth. Often poetic language plays with the world, creating quite new ideas – total lies. Still, they may hold an appeal – a way of transforming the daily, mundane routines into new constructs. How much more interesting if the moon was a balloon (as ee cummings wrote) and drifted around the night skies!

Everyone knows that we should not lie. Setting out to tell a few lies may therefore have an edge. (But just remember: all plays and novels are lies – Shakespeare and Dickens were our greatest liars.) This could be tackled in a straightforward manner by selecting a common subject and listing lies, for example:

Three lies about cottage cheese

1   It is used to pave the roads.
2   Clouds are made of it.
3   The cottages make it look lumpy.

Writing riddles

Riddles are another word for transformation – of lying, disguising, deceiving. We lie to hide the truth. But each part of a good riddle is true enough to act as a clue. Riddles are of course a game – a challenge to unearth what has been disguised. They are one of the oldest and most widespread forms of poetry, and from 'Humpty-Dumpty' onwards writers have been fascinated by them. Many of the riddles that children tell in the playground are hundreds of years old. At the heart of most riddles lies the pleasure we get from disguising one thing as another through creating metaphors. The most famous English medieval riddles are from *The Exeter Book*. This was written about 1,000 years ago, and many of the riddles in it were made up well before that.

Writing 'what' riddles

These riddles are common in playground lore and involve describing what something does in an obscure manner, for example:

- What gets wet when drying? A towel.
- What has six eyes but cannot see? Three blind mice.
- What grows larger the more you take away? A hole in the earth.

To write this sort of riddle take a subject, such as a 'lock'. Now make a list of things about it (e.g. *it holds things in, it needs a key, you can see through it, it is found in a door or window, it can stop people entering somewhere – or escaping*). Take one of these aspects and turn it into a question (e.g. *What keeps you out and yet lets you in?*).

Good subjects for one line 'what' riddles include key, moon, sun, eyes, hand, clock, face, cloud, river, snowflake, cat's-eye, tree, leaf, coin.

Punning riddles

These riddles are built around homophones – words that may sound or be spelled the same but that have different meanings (e.g. *What has an eye but sees nothing? A needle*).

To write these it is useful to work from a list of homophones (e.g. *jam, watch, wave, sink, trip, arms, match, fan, rock, back, light, club, bank, bat, snap, rose*). Take one of the homophones, such as 'watch' or 'bat'. Think of its different meanings:

- A timepiece/to look.
- A flying creature/wooden implement used in cricket.

Then invent a question that suggests both aspects, for example:

- What keeps time and watches it pass by?
- What flies through the night and can score a six?

The mystery guest riddle

These riddles are great fun to write. Choose a person for the riddle (e.g. *My mum*). Think what she, or he, is like – colour, animal, object, place, something from nature, a feeling, a method of transport, a piece if furniture, etc. Once written, others have to guess who the mystery person might be!

She is pink as a marshmallow.
She is a hyena cackling to an audience.
She is a Dresden doll.
She is the River Mersey flowing by.
She is an autumn leaf tumbling down.
She is a gentle dream in which I am lost.
She is a sleek Mercedes, gliding through the town.
She is a comfy sofa, worn at the edges.

This is a very liberating idea – because there is no right or wrong. I first stumbled upon it in a poem by Roger McGough titled 'What You Are'.

You are the cat's paw
Among the silence of midnight goldfish.

It struck me immediately that this might be a liberating writing idea and I first used it with seven- and eight-year-olds. We began by writing a class poem, repeating 'You are...'. We thought of animals, people, places, objects, planets, colours, feelings, dreams. The children then launched into their own versions.

You are the toe nails of a
Fox going silently over the silver moon.
You are the arch way
Standing still over stone steps.
You are the name of a book
Drifting through space
You are the mist caught
On barb-wire screaming for its life.
Hayley, aged 8 years

Later on in the same year we attempted a variation by introducing the idea of describing a person and choosing either 'He is...' or 'She is...'. Once again the idea seemed to release some strong poetry.

She is like a golden star
Slinking into the night.
She is like a flower of light.
She is like a silent pair of lips
Saying something unknown.
She is like a brilliant spurt of love.
She is like an ungrateful silence.
Matthew, aged 7 years

He is in a misty cloud that floats through a
*   bewildered sky.*
He is in swirling smoke that bows at his honour.
He is in a sharp flash of fierce lightning.
He is the sharp blade of a golden knife.
He is a buzzing fly that shimmers in a velvet web.
Tim, aged 8 years

One of the daunting things about working with very young writers is that they can become so good. Their ideas and vision are so fresh – the stale cliché has not quite gripped their language and so it is easier for them to write in new and vital ways. I still think that to write this sort of poetry effectively means to abandon our everyday language and mint a new voice. The writing idea is simple enough and seems so liberating – after all you could write almost anything down. The secret is to try to make each line different or unusual in some way.

Riddles that hide letters

Choose a subject for the riddle, such as 'bug'. Take each letter at a time. Think of a word that contains the first letter and then a word that does not (e.g. *'My first is in table/But never in leg'*). Keep going, hiding all the next letters, for example:

My first is in table
But never in leg.

My second is in umbrella
But never in rain.

My third is in girl
But never in boy.

(bug).

More able writers may choose to use a rhyme, when writing riddles for four- or six-letter words. For instance, a riddle based on the word 'fish' might begin 'My first is in food/ But never in cake'. This opening links the word 'food' and 'cake'. When writing the next couplet, the writer has to use a rhyme (e.g. *'My second is in rain/ But never in lake'*). It helps when writing in this way to select words that rhyme easily.

What am I?

Take a familiar object such as a banana. Brainstorm a list of things that you know about the object – think about its shape, its function, its colour, its taste, what people do with it, think of similes and so forth. For example:

Banana

Boomerang,
Unwrapped present
Rhino horn
Monkeys
Like giant fingers
A bunch of fingers
Some are spotted.

Look at the brainstorm and select a few of the ideas. Use these as clues, extending the ideas into poetic lines. Remember not to give the subject away. The list of clues will use similes and metaphors, for example:

What am I?

I am a soft boomerang,
That will never spin round.
An unwrapped present,
Found far from the ground.
Don't monkey about –
I live in fear of that.

At a glance, I look
Like a giant's yellow fingers,
But the smell that lingers
Is oh, so much sweeter.

Leave me too long
And I'll turn rotten.
Forgotten – and I'll ooze.

Watch out for my skin –
Or you'll lose your step,
And slip flat
On your back
And crack
Your head open.

Pie Corbett

One-line riddles

To write these, all that is needed is one idea – a way of hiding the subject. The following may make a useful starting point for young writers to consider:

- *Golden coin in blue.*
- *Many teeth but no bite.*
- *Ballet dancer accomplishes the splits.*
- *Visionary twins.*
- *Muddying the sky.*
- *One that holds a thousand.*

Pie Corbett

Answers

- Sun
- Comb
- Scissors
- Spectacles
- Clouds
- Seed

Kennings

Kennings act like mini riddles. They are Nordic in origin, and also part of the Anglo-Saxon way of representing objects. Thus the sea was called a 'whale-road'. Intriguingly, this way of describing is very similar to what happens when animals such as orang-utans and monkeys are taught to use sign language. In one such instance, an ape saw a road drill and made the sign for a 'wind hammer'.

The Sea

Whale-road,
Starfish-container,
Cloud-reflector,
Seashore-lapper
Wave-trapper
Rolling-smasher
Moontime-lane.

Pie Corbett

An odd kettle of fish – undermining the cliché

While some forms of poetry adopt the poetic voice, others enjoy exploring the everyday, the clichéd voice that we all inevitably use. Indeed, most speech relies on a very limited vocabulary and is built almost exclusively around the same routines – similar structures constantly repeated.

Idioms are an area that fascinate me. I think it was McGough who wrote 'Her finger has a sadly familiar ring about it'. The possibilities for taking a fresh look at cliché sprung to life. Pete Brown wrote a poem that included the words 'She slammed the door in my face/I opened the door in my face'. There is a whole territory of everyday expression that we use and yet we barely think about its origins or literal meaning. A few simple twists can create simple linguistic jokes. It is almost as if some everyday expressions that we use without a single thought actually hide other layers of possible meaning – the words seem to be saying one thing, but can also mean something else (another form of deception).

The poem on page 58, 'An Odd Kettle of Fish', constituted my first attempt at exploring this technique. I then moved on to a horror version, 'The Poem Imagines it is a Horror Film', which began:

He was so afraid that
He had his heart in his mouth.
(Bloodstains covered his tie.)

I was so angry
That it made my blood boil.
(My brains cooked nicely.)

When she lied
I saw right through her.
(The hole in her head bled.)

My heart sank to my boots.
(But the blood kept my feet warm.)

It's not fair – the teachers
Keep jumping down my throat.
(It makes it hard to breathe.)

A number of other poets picked up on the same idea and the idea began to do the rounds.

To play with this area it is helpful to compile a large collection of everyday sayings and expressions. I find Brewer's *Dictionary of Phrase and Fable* useful. I have provided a short list below for you to use, but this needs further items. My poem provides a simple way of turning expressions on their head and taking them literally, and needs little explanation.

Laugh your head off, Silence is golden, It's raining cats and dogs, As quiet as mice, Over the moon, Her eyes shot round the room, She has her head in the clouds.

A rugby scrum of nuns

The poet David Kitchen has provided a new way of looking at collective nouns (see the poem on page 59). Many of us have had some fun making collections of unusual collective nouns (e.g. *A parliament of owls*) and enjoyed the poetic ring. This invites our own inventions (e.g. *a weariness of teachers, an ogre of Ofsteds*, and so on). David's poem takes this one step further in a topsy-turvy manner that reminds me of Adrian Henri's poem 'Tonight at Noon'.

Read through the poem and provide time for pupils to respond. What has David achieved here? Begin to work on a few examples as a class. Make a list of possible subjects, for example:

- Clouds
- Waves
- Ants
- Glass.

If you want the poem to have a simple rhyme scheme, make sure that the second and fourth ideas rhyme, for example:

- Clouds
- Waves
- Ants
- Graves.

Beside each subject make a quick list of possible 'opposites' that might be used to form collective nouns. The trick is to think about the properties of the subject and then tease out a contradiction or clever link (*a conference of pears*), for example:

- A lead weight of clouds.
- A sandstorm of waves.
- A thunderclap of ants.
- A happiness of graves.

This type of language play would build well on looking at everyday expressions and turning them on their heads (ouch!).

Hiding things in boxes

Probably the best-known model poem for writing is Kit Wright's 'The Magic Box' (page 60). It is one of those few poems that rarely fails to capture the imagination. I provide it here for anyone who has not yet come across it, but also in recognition of its quality as a writing workshop that will activate the imagination.

It is worth spending some time teasing away at the poem itself, discussing each line in turn, looking at what Kit wants to collect in his magic box. Kit uses a range of techniques such as alliteration, swapping ideas around, using unusual, contrasting ideas. The poem shifts from reality towards impossibility. Of course, it provides a simple pattern for writing – What would you put in your box? What is it made of? What would you do with it? This may be added to – Where do you keep it? Where did you find it? Who desires it? Who stole it? And so on.

With some classes it may be helpful to list possible ideas for what might be included. I tend to list ideas under certain headings. For instance, the following categories can act as headings for ideas:

- Birds
- Wild animals
- Domestic pets
- Sea creatures
- Insects
- Colours
- Something you taste, smell, touch, listen to
- A dream
- Something from the country/town

- Something from out of space
- Something from home
- A feeling
- An object doing something impossible
- A lie, secret, wish.

As pupils offer ideas, it can help to show how to take the first thought and make it more interesting by taking it one step further. This may mean seeking a detail. For instance:

- *Tiger* – tiger's eyes – the gleam in a tiger's eye.
- *Elephant* – elephant's tusk – the tip of an elephant's tusk.

The poet Matthew Sweeney has turned the idea on its head by thinking about using the box as a sort of reverse Pandora's box. What sorts of things could we get rid of, could we hide, if we had a box that could contain the horrors of the world? This poem might begin with the small, daily unpleasant details of life (I'd chuck away a migraine) through to the full-scale demons (the time ticking in a terrorist's bomb). Of course, time would need to be spent thinking about how to avoid this becoming a crude list of the 'snot and bogey' type favoured by a few so-called children's poets.

> *Trapped in this box,*
> *Is the time ticking in a terrorist's bomb,*
> *A headache that grips my mind*
> *Like a scarlet band of pain,*
> *A lie as sharp as glass,*
> *The sudden screech of brakes*
> *On wet tarmac –*
> *The cancer that grows*
> *In the night of the body*
> *And remains unknown*
> *For too long –*
> *The turn of a friend*
> *Whose name is rejection,*
> *The word that stings…*
> *Bury this box*
> *Fifteen fathoms deep.*

I have used this alternative idea by lugging into a classroom two boxes. One is a large, crude, wooden box. The other is a carved Indian box with six tiny drawers. What might be trapped inside? In one there is something that I don't like. In the other there is something special. Ideas flow and I jot them down, trying to balance the fine line between a crude list and a list that would touch a nerve. Somehow, having the boxes there stimulates thinking. Often I start by asking the class to jot down several ideas and then share thoughts. Often I prompt, using the checklist of possibilities.

Keeping secrets

Secrets can deceive – they may keep the truth hidden. But poems can unlock the secrets held by experience. It is way of unlocking life. And of course we all love secrets – especially if the secret is someone 'else's. How many times have we heard, 'Now, don't tell anyone else but...' which soon becomes 'I was sworn to deadly secrecy, so whatever you do don't tell anyone else...', 'If she finds out that I've told you, she'll never speak to me again...', and the next thing you know, the secret has done the rounds. Everyone knows that everyone knows except the person who thinks that they hold the secret.

I often start this workshop by asking the class to jot down a secret (one they don't mind others knowing) on a slip of paper. These are put into a hat and then shared out for reading aloud. These can be given a pattern if everyone introduces their secret with some such opening as 'You may not believe it but...'. This means that the result can be read aloud as a group performance.

We discuss secrets. Types of secret – secrets that are meant to be shared. Secrets that are deadly. Dangerous territory so tread carefully.

As a class, look at 'Secret Poem' on page 61. What might the secret be? The poem is acting rather like a riddle but it keeps the secret fast. Tease out the basic structure and imitate:

> *My secret is made*
> *Of....*
>
> *I found it....*
>
> *This secret can....*
>
> *If I lost*
> *This secret....*

An Odd Kettle of Fish

The detectives said that
the books had been cooked.

My teacher said we could
have a free hand.
(I added it to my collection.)

Some people bottle up
their feelings.
(I keep mine in a jar.)

My mother said –
'Hold your tongue!'
(It was too slippery.)

When my sister laughs
she drives me round the bend.
(I catch the bus back.)

Dad told me
to keep a stiff upper lip.
(It's in a box by the bed.)

My uncle is a terrible
name dropper.
(I help my auntie sweep them up.)

Pie Corbett

From *An Odd Kettle of Fish* by John Rice, Pie Corbett and Brian Moses
(Macmillan Children's Books, 1995)

A Fistful of Pacifists

A thimbleful of giants
A rugby scrum of nuns
An atom of elephants
A cuddle of guns

A rustle of rhinoceros
A barrel of bears
A swear box of politicians
A bald patch of hairs

A stumble of ballet dancers
A flutter of whales
A mouthful of silence
A whisper of gales

A pocketful of earthquakes
A conference of pears
A fistful of pacifists
A round-up of squares

David Kitchen

From *Never Play Leapfrog With a Unicorn* (William Heinemann (a division of Reed International) 1995)

The Magic Box

I will put in the box

the swish of a silk sari on a summer night,
fire from the nostrils of a Chinese dragon,
the tip of a tongue touching a tooth.

I will put in the box

a snowman with a rumbling belly,
a sip of the bluest water from Lake Lucerne,
a leaping spark from an electric fish.

I will put in the box

three violet wishes spoken in Gujarati,
the last joke of an ancient uncle
and the first smile of a baby.

I will put in the box

a fifth season and a black sun,
a cowboy on a broomstick
and a witch on a white horse.

My box is fashioned from ice and gold and steel,
with stars on the lid and secrets in the corners.
Its hinges are the toe joints
of dinosaurs.

I shall surf in my box
on the great high-rolling breakers of the wild Atlantic,
then wash ashore on a yellow beach
the colour of the sun.

Kit Wright

From *A Cat Among the Pigeons* (Viking Kestrel 1987)

Secret Poem

My secret is made from –
the fingertips of clouds,
the silence between heartbeats
trapped in a hospital,
the hangman's gloves,
the stoat's bright eye,
the bullet as it slices
through the wind
like the hot knife
slipping through butter.

I found it
on the edge of a lemon's bite,
clutched in the centre of a crocus,
held in a crisp packet,
crumpled at the side of the road
where the nettles stab
their sharp barbs
at the innocent child's
soft, eager hand.

This secret can –
prise open hearts made of steel,
smooth a stormy sea flat,
capture the wind,
cup the moon's shine
in an empty palm,
break apart Mount Everest
till it is powder
in a locket.

If I lost
this secret –
even the lonely goat at the roadside
would bleat . . . .

Pie Corbett

Creating Images – Word Snapshots

Teaching Focus

To experiment with figurative language and form, exploring how form contributes to impact and meaning.

Imagist poetry

The imagists were a group of writers working before the First World War. They believed that the heart of poetry needed clear, sharp images. Their poems are often short, and focus upon illuminating a powerful, central, concrete image – something that can be seen in the reader's mind. The most famous writers were Ezra Pound, Amy Lowell, T.E. Hulme and H.D. I have provided two of my favourite imagist poems, 'In a Station of the Metro' and 'Fog' (see pages 66 and 67).

Faces in the crowd

The first poem is by Ezra Pound. Draw students' attention to the way in which the subject of the poem to be described is stated in the first line and the image in the second, for example:

- Subject: *The crescent moon in the dark night:*
- Image: *Like a scimitar placed on black velvet.*

You may wish to leave the word 'like' out, making the poem more enigmatic – as if the poet is making a comparison but also lining up two different ideas.

> *The crescent moon in the dark night:*
> *a scimitar placed on black velvet.*

One simple way to lead into writing is to write up possible subjects, such as windows, candles, pillows, fingernails, leaves and so on. Then create an image and let it run into a few short lines, for example:

> *Windows:*
> *eyes on the world*
> *whose stare never fails.*

> *Candles:*
> *white, slight figures*
> *on guard all night.*

> *Pillows:*
> *soft wheetabix,*
> *purse of dreams.*

> *Fingernails:*
> *jagged moons*
> *or a fist of suns.*

> *Leaves:*
> *frail maps*
> *marking the road*
> *to nowhere.*

> *Pie Corbett*

Fog

The second poem is another of my favourites. It is so simple and so effective. In this poem the subject is introduced in the first line, then the transforming image 'on little cat feet'. The rest of the poem extends the image further – so the pattern for writing becomes:

- Subject: *The lightning strikes*
- Image: *stabbing the ground.*
- Extend image: *Its yellow blade*
                  crackles electricity.

It can help some young writers if you provide a few opening lines to work from. All they have to do is create the image and extend it further.

> *The snow comes*
> *on white paws*
> *padding so softly,*
> *rubbing its wet nose*
> *against the pane.*

> *The sun comes*
> *shouting about*
> *in the backyard,*
> *blistering skin*
> *with its fiery fingers.*

Haiku, cinquain and counting syllables

Beware of the anorak Haiku hunter

Writing about haiku is a dangerous occupation. It is rather like writing about phonics or grammar. There is always someone who knows better. There is a whole world of haiku specialists out there, just waiting for you to offer a naff definition. If you don't believe me, just check out the number of websites dedicated to haiku.

Log on to George Marsh's haiku website (see Recommended Resources, page 78). Here you will find lesson notes and examples to use, already there waiting to be downloaded. Write to The British Haiku Society (see Recommended Resources) and they will also supply you with lesson ideas and photocopiable sheets with poems to use. I will spend a little time on this area, but cannot recommend too highly these two avenues of practical, cheap support.

I see haiku as a word snapshot – rather like using a few words to take a picture of an image, to create an emotional response. While many struggle to fit the words to a pattern of three lines, 5/7/5 syllables, this does not seem to me necessary. Experiment with haiku of one line, two lines, three lines. Some pupils may enjoy the challenge of counting syllables – the danger is that the poem ends up with the right number of syllables but not capturing the essence of the moment. George Swede, in an illuminating essay, from *Global Haiku*, studies the classical, accepted criteria for writing haiku and alights upon the following principles for today's writers:

1 The haiku must be brief, that is, when read aloud it should be about one breath-length long.
2 The haiku must express a sense of awe or transcendent insight.
3 The haiku must involve some aspect of nature other than human nature.
4 The haiku must possess sense images, not generalisations.
5 The haiku must present an event as happening now, not in the past or future.

One way into haiku is to select a season. List things that you see, hear, taste, smell, touch – typical things that are going on. Try to push beyond cliché at this point. Then use several of these ideas to create a few poetic lines – a little image, for example:

Christmas haiku

Town lights glitter.
Carols drift down the arcade.
Stars are like glass.

Sometimes it helps to provide a final contrasting surprise.

Easter haiku

Blue winds wipe the sky.
Daffodils blossom on High Streets.
So too do Cadbury's cream eggs.

The poems on page 68 are extracts from a holiday diary I keep whenever we go away. Each day I jot down mini moments, just to capture some of the things that happen or I notice. I try to:

- avoid abstractions
- use careful observation
- root the words in the senses
- select each word with care and try out alternatives
- tinker with the word order.

Incidentally, five lines of 5/7/5/7/7 syllables are called 'tanka' and if you write a string of haiku that make up one poem it is called a 'renga'.

Cinquain

I love this form – mainly because it was invented by a lady who had the splendid name of Adelaide Crapsey (not one to forget). This form builds up the poem across five lines, using 2/4/6/8/2 syllables. This will produce a visual pattern as the lines usually grow longer until the last line. It can help to save the last line for some sort of contrast, contradiction, explanation, surprise or emotional punch.

> *Music*
> *Pounding above.*
> *Somebody is dancing*
> *To the disco, of a heart beating*
> *In love.*
>
> Pie Corbett

Englyn

This is a Welsh form of poetry. It has four lines in a pattern of 10/6/7/7 syllables.

Creating pikelets

OK – there is no such form as a pikelet. But I thought that I might invent a short form that creates a pattern on the page, is eight lines long and uses 4/2/4/2/4/2/2/2 syllables. Let your students invent their own forms. Here is a pikelet:

South Downs walkers

Smoke drifts over
chalk hills.
Sunburnt walkers
stalk by;
a distant field
on fire.
Flames climb
higher.

Counting words

As well as forming patterns with syllables, it is also possible to structure poems by counting words. George MacBeth's poem '14 Ways of Touching Peter' has 14 verses. Each verse has 14 words arranged in seven lines. It looks something like this:

You can touch
her slender tail
and let it
run
slowly
between
your fingers.

The possibilities for inventing forms are endless. Counting verses, lines, words, syllables, creating shapes on the page. But none of this means much if the form does not in some way connect with the content of the poem – or if the poem has little to say. Let the poem's meaning dominate – not the form.

Acrostics

This is the form that is too often used for homework in other subjects – it ranks alongside 'do a poster'. Acrostics usually have the letters of the subject written down the page, starting each line, for example:

A scuttling trail of letters;
Never-ceasing, forager;
Tiniest scrap of life.

Using acronyms can be a fun and different way of looking at acrostics. What about a poem based on DIY? (A dictionary helps!) To make this intriguing, spend some time with the class listing words that start with the letter D, then I and finally Y. Then they can put together their ideas from the word bank horizontally, for example:

Dig In Young.
Destroy Ink Yearly.
Dogs Internalise Yams.
Don't Initial Yaks.

A more interesting and less constraining idea is to bury the letters within the poem. In this case I have hidden the answer to the riddle within the poem, for example:

Animal Riddle

Like a small Bear
bundles over the dark road,
brushes pAst the front gate,
as if she owns the joint.
rolls the Dustbin,
like an expert barrel rider
tucks into yesterday's Garbage,
crunches worms for titbits.
wakes us from dEep sleep,
blinks back at torchlight.
our midnight feasteR,
ghost-friend,
moon-lit,
zebra bear.
Pie Corbett

City jungle – metaphor/ personification

This poem (page 69) has a history. I wrote it about 15 years ago, late one night while looking out at the rain lashing the street. The odd motorbike snarled by – cars made their way slowly down the road. Rain goose-pimpled the pavements. The poem came quickly – it basically arrived in one piece and needed only two or three drafts to tighten up the language and play with some internal rhymes.

David Orme used it in his anthology *Toughie Toffee* and hence it found its way into various classrooms. I know teachers who have cut it up and rearranged the lines – then asked the class to reassemble the poem. In this way many different poems can be formed. Some have taken out the verbs and created a cloze procedure. Both are interesting ways in. Discussion roams around the way in which the atmosphere is created. Some tease over the opening 'Rain splinters town', wondering about the word 'splinters'. I seem to recall that this was the first line (the title came at the end, and if I had thought of the title first the poem would have been different). The rain looks like tiny splinters, perhaps shavings of wood flying off a wood turner's wheel – and the rain literally did splinter the view.

I discovered from a friend that it had been used in a GCSE paper. No one sought permission, and to this day I have received nothing. Later on, I was asked if it could be used in the Welsh key stage 2 SATs. I started the bidding at £1,000, but in the end they paid me £150. I wrangled with my conscience – should I take the stance that Adrian Mitchell adopts and not allow my poetry to be used in an exam? Of course, in a sense the horse had already bolted. Besides, part of me was curious about the sort of questions that might be asked. Anyway, if it was good enough for Armitage, it would be good enough for me!

I like to look at this poem as part of a group of three – 'City Jungle', 'Goodnight Stroud' (page 70) and 'Take Two' (page 71).

'Take Two' is the earliest of the three, and the first verse came out of some doodling with collective nouns. I started with 'a bruise of wind', 'a knuckle of rain' ('a stab of sun', 'a punch of thunder', 'a lash of snow', etc.). The second verse arose out of playing about with personification. I imagined a scene and what I could see – a house, trees, a road, the moon, clouds, a dog, shutters banging, an open window, curtains flapping . . . . I then introduced the personification – the shutters bark back (as they 'bang') and the moon coughs discreetly. By the end of the poem 'the stars lose control'. The scene is fading – the poem loses its grip on the world it has created. Again this poem has been used in classrooms and has seen much teasing around the title, 'Take Two'. I was thinking about the second 'take' in a film or recording studio. I was short of a title, wanted something enigmatic, and anyway – the poem was sorted by the second draft!

'Goodnight Stroud' is a homage to my local town. I think that it fits the trio of poems. I was pleased with the internal rhymes and language play (restless as rain./Trains idle up sidelines./ a cyclist sidles by.).

Ask the children to think of the night-time scene they are going to write about. They should note down the key elements that are in the scene. In 'Goodnight Stroud', I noted in my journal clock tower, streets, Belisha beacon, taxis, bus, etc. Take each idea and embellish it, using personification, simile, alliteration and so on.

In a Station of the Metro

The apparition of these faces in a crowd;

Petals on a wet, black bough.

Ezra Pound

From *Personae* (Faber 1924)

Fog

The fog comes
on little cat feet.
It sits looking
over harbour and city
on silent haunches
and then moves on.

Carl Sandburg

From *Chicago Poems* (Harcourt Brace 1944)

From *'Spain, Summer 2001 – Poetry Diary'*

Wednesday morning.

Cicadas buzz
like electricity.

It's so hot that
wasps and bees drink
from the swimming pool.

Ants carry off
trophies from our meal.

Stunned by sun.
Heat bounces
off whitewashed walls.
The track ahead shimmers.

Flies irritate –
whining,
stalking the cup's rim –
settling on my hand.

Towels slung
in the breeze.
A distant lorry tugs up hill.

Cicadas are busy.
The hillside seems alive.
Inside, the fridge hums too.
The landscape does nothing
too.

clouds   drift   my thoughts

Distant hills –
like a sleeping lion
crouch.

The sun steadily
turns up the temperature.

Pastel blue dragonflies, pencil-slim,
hover by the pool.

Daisy's wasp sting –
white injection mark –
like a raised moon.

It's 3 o'clock at night.
Lightning bursts over mountains
in a purple fuzz.

Trying to sleep but
the room is too stuffy –
even the pillows sweat.

Moon crumbles   night swim
stars scatter

Pie Corbett

City Jungle

Rain splinters town.

Lizard cars cruise by;
their radiators grin.

Thin headlights stare –
shop doorways keep
their mouths shut.

At the roadside
hunched houses cough.

Newspapers shuffle by,
hands in their pockets.
The gutter gargles.

A motorbike snarls;
dustbins flinch.

Streetlights bare
their yellow teeth.
The motorway's
cat-black tongue
lashes across
the glistening back
of the tarmac night.

Pie Corbett

From *Rice, Pie and Moses* (Macmillan Children's Books 1995)

Goodnight Stroud

The Clock Tower glowers.
Its hands fidget towards dawn.
Dark streets yawn.

It's late.
The streets wait,
restless as rain.

Trains idle up sidelines.
A cyclist sidles by.

Black taxis scuttle
down back alleys.
A bright bus blunders
up the High Street.

The belisha beacon blinks.
Parked cars huddle
like wet toads.
The night thinks
that the stars
are sending morse-code.

Pie Corbett

From *The Apple Raid* (Macmillan Children's Books 2001)

Take Two

A bruise of wind
fists the street;
a knuckle of rain
punches south.

The shutters bark
back and the moon
coughs discreetly.

The fog busies itself
up some clipped alleyway.

Night nibbles dawn.

The stars lose control.

Pie Corbett

From *The Apple Raid* (Macmillan Children's Books 2001)

Playing With Rhyme

Teaching Focus

To experiment with rhythm, rhyme and form.

Free verse and rhymes

Somewhere along the line you are going to introduce the idea of free verse and look at the use of rhyme. Let us start with free verse. To put it simply, free verse is poetry that does not use any regular syllabic, metrical or rhyming pattern. It is built around the flow of speech and is given a pattern on the page that may suggest pauses, or give emphasis to certain words or lines. Free verse does not lean upon anyone else's structure. Look no further than the poetry of D.H. Lawrence to find superb examples.

Much of the poetry that young writers create will fall into the category of free verse. If we follow Ted Hughes' idea of writing rapidly, in a meditative flow and acquire the skill of listening to our inner voice then free verse will flow.

Rhyme is another matter. It is not easy to control, and needs a skilled and practised writer to handle it effectively. Let us pause and think about this. If I provided you with a pile of wood and some carpentry tools, could you make me a Welsh dresser? The answer is probably not. And if I was teaching you carpentry we would not start with Welsh dressers! There are skills to acquire – how to measure, cut, create joins, plane and so forth.

Poetry is the same. It seems to me that there are skills to hone – learning to observe, watching the world, wondering, imagining. The ability to select words with care, sifting synonyms – and then weighing their impact. Drawing on an ever-increasing poetic base – using alliteration, onomatopoeia, simile, metaphor, personification and so forth. Rhyming is hard if the vocabulary is limited and the writer cannot draw rapidly upon a larger pool of words than everyday speech.

Let us look at different sorts of rhyme and then some ideas for beginning to develop skill with handling it without descending into nonsense.

- *Full rhymes* rhyme completely – kill, fill, ill, pill.
- *Half rhymes* almost rhyme – blade, blood, brood.
- *Eye rhymes* are words that look as if they should rhyme but do not – near, pear.
- *Internal rhymes* – where the rhyme does not fall at the end of the line but within the poem (see 'Goodnight Stroud', page 70).

Couplets

Rhyming couplets can offer a fun way into using rhyme, especially where the concept is playful. For instance, the poet Adrian Henri wrote a poem called 'You Make Me Feel' which is basically a list of similes in rhyming couplets. Of course, for it to work the metre needs to be regular as well. This can be made easier by repeating the lines as you write so that they 'fit' – they sound the same. Here is a starter:

> *You make me feel like a pound of peas*
> *You make me feel like shaking my knees.*

Limericks

There are a few forms or patterns where rhyme can be practised – limericks are one of the best known, usually on the back of the slightly dodgy! But beware: they are not easy to write. Try using place names, for example:

> *There was a young man from Stroud*
> *Whose ties were especially loud.*
> *The colours were bright*
> *And lit up the night,*
> *Which made him stand out in a crowd.*

Sonnets, ballads and all that stuff

A few young writers will want to tackle other forms – ballads, boustrophedons, double dactyls, pantoums, rondels, sestinas, sonnets, triolets and villanelles. My own experience is that more demanding forms which may use a distinctive rhyming pattern are usually too hard for most young writers. The form dominates and the content is too often sacrificed. Those who are interested should look at Andrew Peter's useful little anthology *The Unidentified Frying Omelette*, which provides examples of different forms and a useful glossary.

Most young writers need to learn first to observe the detail of experience, to play with words and ideas, to create new and truthful combinations, to select language with care, to generate ideas and words rapidly .... To begin to become writers. There is plenty of time to build upon such foundations and tackle more demanding forms later on.

Stufferation

This poem by Adrian Mitchell has been a favourite since I saw him perform it with such gusto at the Cheltenham Literature Festival many years ago. The format is quite simple. Here is one verse:

Harps are strung with it
Mattresses are sprung with it
Wire
I like that stuff

> Adrian Mitchell, from *Greatest Hits*
> (Bloodaxe, 1991)

Adrian's poem is about things that he likes – Roger McGough used the same format some years ago to write about things that he hates. Either way round it works well.

Using rhyme is not easy, and for young writers a pattern such as this one provides the challenge of using rhyme within a safe cell. I like to begin by reading the poem aloud, rhythmically and powerfully – letting the poem rip a bit. This can be followed by pupils' responses. Move into writing by listing likes/dislikes.

Tease away at the pattern before modelling a few verses with the whole class. Basically, the poem always ends with 'I like that stuff' or 'I hate that stuff' as the fourth line. The third line is the name of the stuff in question. Easy – half a verse written and no thought required!

The first two lines act as clues. Rather like a riddle. The other added factor is attempting to rhyme the lines. At first do not worry about the rhyme – push for a decent opening line that acts as a clue. For instance, if the last two lines read as follows:

Eggs
I hate that stuff.

the first line needs to suggest the subject. Come up with a few ideas about eggs – Humpty-Dumpty, chickens, boxes of six, needed for omelettes, look bald and so on. Work out an opening line, using a similar rhythm to the original poem (e.g. 'Chickens lay them'). Now the tough bit is to find a rhyming line (e.g. 'Shops display them'). Note where the rhyme lies. If you cannot find a rhyme then change the opening line.

Chickens lay them,
Shops display them.
Eggs.
I hate that stuff.

Trees covered in it.
The grass gets smothered in it.
Leaves.
I like that stuff.

Teachers enjoy it.
Loudmouths destroy it.
Peace.
I like that stuff.

Nursery rhymes rewritten

I think it was Sandy Brownjohn who first introduced me to the teasing game of rewriting nursery rhymes through one of her excellent source books (see Recommended Resources). The task is to take a well-known nursery rhyme and rewrite it without using the letter 'e'. This is harder than it sounds and makes a teasing linguistic game.

Nursery rhymes offer a strong structure for innovation. Innovation is where you take a well-known text and alter it slightly. There is a strong pedigree of this in narrative where familiar fairy-tales such as 'The Three Little Pigs' have been rewritten in different settings, with different characters or from another angle. Some playground rhymes have taken well-known rhymes or pop songs and innovated on the text. I still recall singing as a child, 'We four kings of Liverpool are, George in a taxi, John in a car/ Paul on his scooter/ Tooting his hooter/ Following Ringo Starr'.

Take a well-known rhyme and begin by crossing out some parts and making slight alterations, for example:

Little Miss Muffet	Little Miss Dare
Sat on a tuffet	Sat on a chair
Eating her curds and whey	Eating some baked beans on toast
There came a big spider	There came an old crook
Who sat down beside her	Who read her a book
And frightened Miss Muffett away.	And now she loves him the most.

It does help to make a list of well-known nursery rhymes, songs, carols, hymns, pop songs, and so on. Some children may make only minor changes – others will be confident enough to take the rhythm and alter the words completely.

Art and Poetry

Paintings, postcards and sculptures

Jan Mark introduced me to the idea of using postcards of paintings as a way into writing narrative many years ago. Her game was to pretend that the postcard that had been chosen was the illustration in the middle of a novel. The pupils had to write the facing page. The advantage of this technique was that the children's concentration shifted from plot to a more careful consideration of writing a scene.

I began to build up my collection immediately and now have several hundred that I use on a regular basis. Those that work best include portraits, paintings of scenes, anything by Stanley Spencer, Edward Burra, surrealists (especially Dali), photos of black jazz musicians and so on. Every time I visited a gallery I would buy another dozen and in this way the collection keeps being added to. It is always interesting that children tend to choose certain paintings again and again.

I spread the cards out and ask them to choose a postcard which contains an image that seems to speak to them, that has some possibilities, that intrigues and interests. We then turn our attention to a poster-size painting. A large Van Gogh will do – but anything that is to hand. I use this to demonstrate how to build up a poem about a painting.

Building the poem

Begin by listing down the centre of the page the main details that can be seen in the painting. If we are looking at a portrait such as Stanley Spencer's *Self-portrait* we might write:

Eyes

Hair

Lips

Brow

Make sure that the list of details is placed in the middle of the board and leave space between each detail. Take each detail in turn and demonstrate how to flesh out the word, adding either side to create a list of poetic sentences. For example, you might begin by adding an adjective in front of eyes and then extending the sentence:

Brown eyes bulge and stare like glass marbles.

Hair

Lips

Brow

Most young writers will work on each detail in turn. If they get stuck on one, they should move on. Details may be dropped and others added in. It is helpful to draw attention to a checklist of possible stylistic devices. You could use well-chosen adjectives, powerful verbs, alliteration, similes, metaphors, personification. Try to aim for at least one surprise in each line.

When writing, the first thought is not always the best thought. For instance, when looking at a postcard of a sunset Jamie wrote, 'The sunset spotted by red'. He then thought further and decided that 'red' was too easy, too obvious. He tried the idea of 'red lava' but was still unhappy with 'red' – after all, most lava is some shade of red and it still felt too obvious. Suddenly he thought of a cockerel's tail feathers and angry plume. This gave him 'The sunset spotted by cockerel lava'. A unique image, using a noun as an adjective.

It is worth pursuing this idea of 'the first thought is not always the best thought' when revising. Which words can be fine-tuned? Where can a more powerful and potent combination of words be found? This does not mean 'bigger' words, such as changing 'sad' for 'morose'. It is about finding the right combination, one that illuminates the subject, and surprises the reader with a new insight.

When collecting ideas it is worth jotting down the word 'like' in big letters to add to the list of similes: What do the eyes look like? – eggs, marbles, moons, suns, planets, crumpets. These may be used as similes or to show the shift from simile into metaphor by crossing out the word 'like' (e.g. 'brown eyes like planets', 'brown eyes are planets'). Demonstrate how to extend the metaphor – What do planets do? 'Brown eyes drift like planets lost in the universe.'

The Poker Room
(after a painting by Edward Burra)

The knife lies motionless in the murky room.
The hand quivers, a sudden crash,
A streak of lightning stuns the silent sky.
A breeze blown, the cigarette smoke streaks
In a misty haze out through the door.
The table shudders as the stranger reaches
For the dusty gin bottle.
The carved, silent ring presents-
An omen.
A crumpled week old paper
Floats to the ground.
Blurred dots of the dice roll
To show a six.
The stranger cackles,
Startling.

Clare, Year 7

The Rooster and the Hen
(after a painting by Ito Jakuchu)

The tree is a dragon.
Red stems are blazing fire.
The feathers are a wild snake.
Their smooth layers are ridged scales.
The crown of the rooster rocks unsteadily
Like the blade of a whisker.

Long strips of grass lie scattered
Among the sharp, uneven daggers.
Clustered leaves shake,
Crisp veins of the unknown.

Active eyeballs alert,
Straining the minute bead.

Shaded berries burst beneath nimble bones.
The rooster struts nearby.
Deep pale beds overlap
The shelter of the mushroom.

Natalie, Year 7

Music

Using music as a starting point is perhaps a somewhat hackneyed idea, recalling some of the most derided teaching of the 1960s and 1970s – the kaftanned, perfumed excesses of creativity that became the beating stick used by the likes of Chris Woodhead. However, I can still recall the day some 35 years ago when my English teacher Peter Pollard asked us to listen to some classical music – something from *The Planets* I think – and just let our minds wander, noting down images, ideas, words, anything that drifted by. We listened, dreamed and noted for about ten minutes.

I was amazed to see I had covered about four pages with words, in patterns. We then spent a further 20 minutes shaping the writing. Using a numbering technique helped to break the flow of language into sections that seemed to reflect the changing mood of the music. It meant little but was a stimulating and potent method for limbering up the words, exploring possibilities.

1   *Distant hills crouch –*
    Lions waiting to pounce,
    Sleepy giants.

2   *Hunger is a wolf,*
    Prowling the edges of the world.
    Sniffing out the last chance saloon,
    Waiting for the weak.

3   *Wishes –*
    Goldfish scales
    Gleam.
    The sudden scent
    Of a hyacinth.
    Throwing a promise
    Into a well –
    And catching
    Only the echo
    Of a splash.

4   *Poppies like so many thousand parachutes.*
    Tiny frail frisbees –
    Paper-thin tissue.
    Blood-red reminders.

Sculpture

In August 2000 I was invited by Scholastic Press to visit Tate Modern with the poets Brian Moses and Valerie Bloom. We were given the challenge of writing a poem by 3 p.m., to be based on any sculpture that grabbed our interest. The results would be published in one of their educational magazines plus a reflection of the experience.

We wandered around, making a note of different possibilities. Brian decided early on to write about the giant spider and Val chose a strange-looking construction that resembled an igloo made of broken shards of glass. I chose Dali's *Lobster Telephone*. A photographer arrived and took various pictures of me standing by the phone. (In the end the magazine used a photo of me staring through the perspex casing, with various reflections looking rather like a mad surrealist.)

By lunchtime I was wedged between Val and Brian in the cafeteria. They were both well into their poems, scribbling madly. I sat there with that awful feeling that everyone else was writing, 'inspired', and I did not have a clue. I wrote in my journal:

> In the end I chose the 'Lobster Telephone' because it is so memorable and I think that it would appeal to children. How might other everyday objects be transformed? I imagined a car with sunflowers for wheels, a wall light with an ice-cream cornet for a bulb, a dog with a snake for a collar, or thumbs instead of chimney pots! The possibilities seemed endless.
>
> I wanted to write something simple that children could imitate. My initial idea was to invent a repeating line, so that the writer could transform the world in the same surreal manner, e.g.

> *In the surreal world I travelled in*
> *A Mercedes with sunflower wheels.*
>
> *In the surreal world I turned on*
> *A light to be met by an ice-cream cone that*
> *   glowed.*
>
> *In the surreal world I passed*
> *A dog with a snake collar that hissed at me.*
>
> *In the surreal world I saw*
> *Chimney pots giving the thumbs up.*

However, the poem I spent most of my time working on was based on the idea of the phone ringing and there being a lobster on the line. I listed a range of things that were not on the line, using a rhyming pattern with a brief refrain to hold the poem together. I tried to end on an ominous note. After all, when the phone starts turning into a lobster all may not be well!

We began writing whilst waiting for lunch. I was squashed between Val and Brian. Brian had already started. Val was busy covering her page with notes. All I had was the title. Panic set in – *I couldn't think of anything, I was behind already, time was ticking by. . . .* The empty page stared up at me. Then the opening line came to me, out of nowhere, so I followed it like a tracker dog.

Who's That on the Phone?

(after 'Lobster Telephone' by Salvador Dali)

There's a lobster on the phone!
Not a crayfish
Or a seal,
Not a spider crab
Or an eel –
But a lobster!

Not a mobster
Full of threats,
Nor debt collector
seeking debts –
But a lobster!

Not a salesgirl,
Double-glazing,
Nor astrologer,
future-grazing –
But a lobster!

Not an emu
On the loose,
Nor a zebra,
Nor a moose,
Not a hangman
With a noose . . . .

No, there's a lobster on the phone
And he wants to speak to you!

Pie Corbett

Looking back, I see that under pressure I fell back on a useful technique – when in doubt use a repeating pattern. I remember Ralph Wood writing about an African necklace made of large stone beads. He tried to describe the beads but then found that there was little to say. I suggested that he might find a repeating line and use that. In the end he alighted on a counting pattern:

> *One is a stone heart.*
> *Two is a chicken's bright eye.*
> *Three is an egg imprisoning a thought.*
> *Four is a thought like a planet stuck in the mind.*

Some pupils will be able to invent their own repeating patterns, others may need you to make some suggestions. For instance, I once took a class to see a Henry Moore sculpture and we experimented with the following three ideas that could be used as repeating lines:

- *The hole in my mind sees . . . .*
- *In this curve I saw . . . .*
- *The empty soul needs . . . .*

The work of the artist Andy Goldsworthy is worth exploring as an inspiration to students interested in taking their creative thinking a few steps further. Ian Hamilton Finlay is well known for his garden in Scotland where he has poems carved into stone and set into shapes. Goldsworthy has an interesting sequence of photographs where he uses autumn leaves to create patterns. Leaves might be dampened and plastered into words against a dull background. Yellow or red leaves make the most interesting contrast. Colour photos taken with a digital camera can mean that everyone in the class can soon have the image run off the computer.

Recommended Resources

Websites

I have just included a few essential sites – there are thousands all over the world about writing, for writers and readers. This is just a beginning.

For teachers

- George Marsh's haiku site: George used to work in teaching and writes himself. There are sample lessons ready to be downloaded and haiku to be used in class. Superb stuff. www.haiku.insouthsea.co.uk George's site has a link to a site run by Martin Alan Osterhaus which contains every decent link you ever needed for those interested in haiku.
- The National Association of Writers in Education: this site contains some excellent poetry written by children arising from different writing projects plus useful articles by writers, many containing workshop approaches – invaluable. www.nawe.co.uk
- The Poetry Book Society: this site links you into the society that can keep you up to date with the best in poetry publishing. There are useful poetry packs for teachers/posters, etc. A must for poetry enthusiasts and should be on every department's list. www.poetrybooks.co.uk
- The Poetry Society: the society is another must for every department. Martin Colthorpe (020 7420 9894 or email on education@poetrysoc.com) is currently their education contact. He will discuss and advise on such issues as inviting poets into schools. Over the years the society has produced many excellent packs and books. Young writers who are really interested may wish to take up Poetry Society youth membership. www.poetrysoc.com
- Poetry Class: this Poetry Society site provides information about having a poet to run in-service in schools and provides a wonderful bank of poetry workshop ideas. No one should be short of creative techniques with this sort of support to hand. Funded by the DfES, this is a good example of imaginative government approaches to supporting literacy. www.poetryclass.net
- Apples and Snakes are based primarily in London. Talk to Nicky Crabb on 020 7924 3410 if you are interested in having a writer in school. The site provides useful information on fund raising and having writers in school. Lively – a definite site to check. www.applesandsnakes.org
- The Poetry Library: this is the site/place to go as they house just about every poetry book that has been published. Useful for research, competitions and events, teaching materials, etc. Check it out. www.poetrylibrary.org.uk
- Stone Soup: this site provides excellent links on to other sites for young writers – also useful materials for teachers. www.stonesoup.com

For children

Give the web addresses of these sites out to every child:

- Young Writer: this is the home site of the magazine for children interested in writing – interviews with writers, chances to publish, writing competitions, writing tips, etc. – excellent. www.mystworld.com/youngwriter
- The Poetry Zone: the best poetry site for children in this country. Teaching materials, interviews, publish your own – it is lively, bouncy and brilliant for children and teachers. www.poetryzone.ndirect.co.uk

Books, reading materials and courses

I have listed these books in order. If you read all of these then you need look no further – other than your own ability to invent, to seek out new avenues, to write yourself. You could treat these books like a large workshop on how to teach poetry writing.

1 Books about teaching writing poetry

- *Poetry in the Making*, Ted Hughes (Faber). This book lays the foundations.
- *Jumpstart – Poetry in the Secondary School*, Cliff Yates (The Poetry Society). Excellent, creative manual by an inspiring teacher of poetry.
- *Sing Me Creation*, Paul Matthews (Hawthorn Press). A wonderful source of creative ideas.
- *To Rhyme or not to Rhyme?*, Sandy Brownjohn (Hodder and Stoughton). Another essential resource by a talented teacher of poetry.
- *How to Write*, John Moat and John Fairfax (Elm Tree Books). This is very strong on making sense of grammar in relation to writing.
- *Creating Writers* and *Talking Books*, both by